Fuzzy Logic Based Categorical Text Clustering in Data Mining

Dr.S.M. Jagatheesan,

Associate Professor of Computer Science,

PG & Research Department of Computer Science,

Gobi Arts & Science College (Autonomous), Gobichettipalayam.

Dr. V. Thiagarasu,

Associate Professor of Computer Science,

PG & Research Department of Computer Science

Gobi Arts & Science College (Autonomous), Gobichettipalayam.

Published by

Fuzzy Logic Based Categorical Text Clustering in Data Mining

ISBN 978-93-86638-81-6

Authors

Dr.S.M. Jagatheesan
Dr.V. Thiagarasu

Bonfring
309, 2nd Floor, 5th Street Extension, Gandhipuram,
Coimbatore-641 012.
Tamilnadu, India.
E-mail: info@bonfring.org
Website: www.bonfring.org
Phone: 0422 4213231

Acknowledgements

We would like to express our sincere gratitude to many people who help to bring this book in a fruit full one. We would like to present our deep sense of gratitude and sincere thanks to Gobi Arts & Science College Management and the Principal **Dr.R. SELLAPPAN**, for the encouragement and support to complete this book.

Authors

Dr.S.M. Jagatheesan

Dr.V. Thiagarasu

I would like to extend my special thanks to my dedicated wife **Mrs. J. REVATHY**, my blessed sons **Er. S.J. JIVITESH** and **Mr. S.J. SANJITH** and my beloved mother **Mrs. M.PALANIAMMAL** for their support, encouragement, help and cooperation to complete the book.

Dr.S.M. Jagatheesan

Preface

Data mining is a process of retrieving useful information from a large set of databases based on the queries and the source of information collected from various fields such as science, business and engineering and it encloses a multifaceted process, from data preparation to knowledge representation. There are various data mining algorithms and techniques which uses tools that examine the unknown pattern along with the association of data. Data mining consists of various tasks such as classification, clustering and association rules. The text clustering is a process based on the query given by the user and information retrieval from a large database which undergoes several processes like preprocessing, extracting and filtering. A real-time example is that a web search responds to a user query after analyzing thousands of web pages and the major difficulty in this process is identifying the accurate page. To overcome this problem, clustering approach enables automatic grouping of related pages based on the user search. But the process of grouping relevant pages is difficult without changing the meaning. This drawback leads to delay of services in terms of data mining and motivates to find an algorithm to identify the semantically related sentences and to avoid duplication on the given data set.

The method of categorizing the text data is a major task in the information retrieval and brief survey on optimization approaches to text document clustering was carried out which limits to provide clustering on semantics to improve the quality of text clustering. Different existing text mining algorithms are briefly reviewed and the four categorical data mining techniques such as the k-modes, ROCK [Robust Clustering using links], STIRR [Sieving Through Iterated Relational Reinforcement] and the fuzzy algorithms are discussed.

The clustering accuracy and efficiency were discussed on sentence level clustering using fuzzy logic. Each technique has different usages which were used on data set first and the best method in each technique has been noted and used for global comparison with other techniques for the same data set. An efficient approach for mining complete sets of frequent item sets was presented by constructing a tree structure with possible frequent k-itemsets. A query redirection method has been proposed to improve the k-means clustering algorithm performance and accuracy. To overcome the limitations in the k-means algorithm, k-modes algorithm has been developed because k-means algorithm does not support categorical data. It measures the dissimilarities between the two nodes and also minimizes the cost functions. The k-mode algorithm is not applicable for processing wide range of inputs which is a major limitation and also it requires in-memory operations. The ROCK is a robust hierarchical clustering algorithm which employs links and not distances when merging clusters. This method extends non-metric similarity measures and cluster with the categorical attributes which produce quality cluster rather than the traditional approaches. The ROCK algorithm still lacks efficiency in determining the quality of the similarity measures. STIRR is an effective algorithm that clusters the attribute values and it is efficient in processing intra-attribute value clustering. The limitation of STIRR is only one dataset can pass over it and requires a linear number of in-memory for processing the dataset operations

The categorical text clustering increases the efficiency during the informational retrieval for the user query and it reduces the time consumption on data mining with the objective of a meaningful text.

The text book is designed for everyone who wants to learn the concepts of data mining, data mining techniques, basics of data warehousing, and fuzzy logic approaches to data mining.

Objectives of the Book

The book is designed to learn about the data mining, data mining techniques and data warehousing. The book describes about Information Retrieval & Knowledge Discovery and discusses about the various types of clustering algorithms. It describes the importance of text clustering methods.

This book explains about the method to design and development of an algorithm based on fuzzy logic approach to have effective categorical text clustering and to reduce time complexity. Finally, it discusses the various recent trends in Fuzzy Based Clustering Algorithm.

Organization of the Book

This book is organized in the following chapters.

The chapter 1 specifies the basics concepts of data mining, description of various data mining techniques such as Decision Trees, Sequential Pattern, Clustering, Predictive Data Mining, Association Rule Mining, and Classification. Also it contains basics of data warehouse, architecture of data warehouse and its applications.

The chapter 2 discuss about the information retrieval and knowledge discovery in database, data mining models which includes Clustering, Classification, and Associate Mining in Database. Also it describe about various clustering algorithms, their comparison and applications of clustering analysis.

The chapter 3 explains about text clustering methods viz. Frequent Term Based Text Clustering, Apriori Method, and Frequent Pattern-Growth Method, Sentence Level Clustering. This chapter also analysis of the following Text Clustering Methods: K-Means and K-Modes Methods, Fuzzy K-Modes Method, ROCK and STIRR Algorithm.

The chapter 4 describes about fuzzy based modeling, Fuzzy Machine Learning, Fuzzy Decision Trees, Fuzzy Prototype, Fuzzy Clustering, Fuzzy Logic, Fuzzy Inference System, and Fuzzy Clustering Techniques.

The chapter 5 discusses about the recent trends in fuzzy based clustering algorithm, Fuzzy Categorical Clustering, Design of Attributes, Clustering Famous Quotation, Measuring sentence similarity, and recent trends in fuzzy. This chapter also describes the Fuzzy Based Architectural Design and Architectural Design.

Bibliography

CHAPTER 1

DATA MINING AND WAREHOUSING

1.1. Data Mining

Data mining is a process of automatically searching large stores of data to discover patterns and trends that go beyond simple analysis. Data mining uses sophisticated mathematical algorithms to segment the data and evaluate the probability of future events and it is also known as Knowledge Discovery in Data (KDD). The key properties of data mining are:

- Automatic discovery of patterns
- Prediction of likely outcomes
- Creation of actionable information
- Focus on large data sets and databases

The key data mining processes are:

- Data cleaning (remove noise and inconsistent data)
- Data integration (combination of multiple data sources)
- Data selection (where data relevant to the analysis task are retrieved from the database)
- Data transformation (where data are transformed and consolidated into forms appropriate for mining by performing summary or aggregation operations)
- Data mining (an essential process where intelligent methods are applied to extract data patterns)
- Pattern evaluation
- Knowledge presentation (where visualization and knowledge representation techniques are used to present mined knowledge to users)

Data mining is a very important process which is potentially useful and previously unknown information that is extracted from large volumes of data. There are a number of components involved in the data mining process and these components constitute the architecture of a data mining system.

Data Mining Architecture

The major components of any data mining system are *data source, data warehouse server, data mining engine, pattern evaluation module, graphical user interface* and *knowledge base.*

Data Source

Database, data warehouse, World Wide Web (www), text files and other documents are the actual sources of data and there is a need for large volumes of historical data for data mining to be successful. Organizations usually store data in databases or data warehouses. Data warehouses may contain one or more databases, text files, spreadsheets or other kinds of information repositories. Sometimes, data may reside even in plain text files or spreadsheets. World Wide Web or the Internet is another big source of data.

Different Processes

The data needs to be cleaned, integrated and selected before passing it to the database or data warehouse server. As the data is from different sources and in different formats, data should not be used directly for the data mining process because the data might not be complete and reliable. So, first data needs to be cleaned and integrated. Again, more data to be collected from different data sources and only the required data~~ of interest~~ needs to be selected and passed to the server. These processes are not as simple as one think. A number of techniques to be performed on the data as part of cleaning, integration and selection.

Database or Data Warehouse Server

The database or data warehouse server contains the actual data that is ready to be processed. Hence, the server is responsible for retrieving the relevant data based on the request of the user.

Data Mining Engine

The data mining engine is the core component of any data mining system and it consists of a number of modules for performing data mining tasks including association, classification, characterization, clustering, prediction, time-series analysis etc.

Pattern Evaluation Modules

The pattern evaluation module is mainly responsible for the measure of interestingness of the pattern by using a threshold value and it interacts with the data mining engine to focus the search towards interesting patterns.

Graphical User Interface

The graphical user interface module communicates between the user and the data mining system. This module helps the user to use the system easily and efficiently without knowing the real complexity behind the process. When the user specifies a query or a task, this module interacts with the data mining system and displays the result in an easily understandable manner.

Knowledge Base

The knowledge base is helpful in the whole data mining process and it might be useful for guiding the search or evaluating the interestingness of the result patterns. The knowledge base might even contain user beliefs and data from user experiences that can be useful in the process of data mining. The data mining engine might get inputs from the knowledge base to make the result more accurate and reliable. The pattern evaluation module interacts with the knowledge base on a regular basis to get inputs and also to update it.

Data Mining Workspace

The Mining software examines the patterns and relationships based upon the open ended user queries stored in transaction data. The workspace consists of four types of work relationships such as *clusters, classes, Sequential Patterns and Associations.*

- **Clusters:** The clustering is a known grouping of data items according to logical relationships and users priority. For instance, the data can be extracted to identify user affinities as well as market sections.
- **Classes:** Data is used to locate the predetermined groups. For instance, a store could locate the customer data to examine customer's visit and their purchasing. This information helps to increase the customer traffic at store.
- **Sequential Patterns:** Data Mining is used to forecast the behaviour trends and patterns of market.
- **Associations:** Associative mining is used to locate associations such as beer-diaper instance.

1.2. Data Mining Techniques

Several major mining techniques are discussed below:

- **Decision Trees:** It is the most common technique used for data mining because of its simplest structure. The decision tree in data mining serves as a condition or question with multiple answers. Each answer leads to specific data that help us to determine final decision based upon it.
- **Sequential Patterns:** The pattern analysis used to discover regular events, similar patterns in transaction data. Like, in sales; the historical data of customers helps us to

identify the past transactions in a year. Based on the historic purchasing frequency of customer, the best deals or offers have been introduced by business firms.

- **Clustering:** Using the automatic method, cluster of objects is formed having similar characteristics. By using clustering, classes are defined and then suitable objects are placed in each class.
- **Prediction:** This method discovers the relationship between independent and dependent instances. For example, in the area of sales; to predict the future profit, sale acts as independent instance and profit could be dependent. Then based on historical data of sales and profit, associated profit is predicted.
- **Association:** Also called relation technique, in this a pattern is recognized based upon the relationship of items in a single transaction and it is a suggested technique for market basket analysis to explore the products that customer frequently demands.
- **Classification:** Based upon machine learning, classification is used to classify each item in a particular set into predefined groups. This method adopts mathematical techniques such as neural networks, linear programming, and decision trees and so on.

1.2.1. Decision Trees

A decision tree is a graph that uses a branching method to illustrate every possible outcome of a decision. Decision trees can be drawn by hand or created with a graphics program or specialized software. Informally, decision trees are useful for focusing discussion when a group must make a decision. Programmatically, they can be used to assign monetary/time or other values to possible outcomes so that decisions can be automated. Decision tree software is used in data mining to simplify complex strategic challenges and evaluate the cost-effectiveness of research and business decisions. Variables in a decision tree are usually represented by circles.

A **decision tree** is a graphical representation of possible solutions to a decision based on certain conditions. It is called a decision tree because it starts with a single box (or root), which then branches off into a number of solutions, just like a tree.

Decision trees are helpful, not only because they are graphics that help to 'see' what one is thinking, but also because making a decision tree requires a systematic, documented thought process. Often, the biggest limitation of the decision making is that one can only select from the known alternatives. Decision trees help formalize the brainstorming process so that one can identify more potential solutions.

An example: An email management decision tree might begin with a box labeled "Receive new message." From that, one branch leading off might lead to "Requires immediate response." From there, a "Yes" box leads to a single decision: "Respond." A "No" box leads to "Will take less than three minutes to answer" or "Will take more than three minutes to answer." From the first box, a box leads to "Respond" and from the second box, a branch leads to "Mark as task and assign priority." The branches might converge after that to "Email responded to? File or delete message."

Decision Tree Induction

Decision tree induction is the learning of decision trees from class-labeled training tuples. A decision tree is a flowchart-like tree structure, where each internal node (non-leaf node) denotes a test on an attribute, each branch represents an outcome of the test, and each leaf node (or terminal node) holds a class label. The topmost node in a tree is the root node. A typical decision tree is shown in Figure 1.1. and it represents the concept buys computer, that is, it predicts whether a customer at All electronics is likely to purchase a computer. Internal nodes are denoted by rectangles, and leaf nodes are denoted by ovals. Some decision tree algorithms produce only binary trees (where each internal node branches to exactly two other nodes), whereas others can produce non binary trees. "How are decision trees used for classification?". Given a tuple, X, for which the associated class label is unknown, the attribute values of the tuple are tested against the decision tree. A path is traced from the root to a leaf node, which holds the class prediction for that tuple. Decision trees can easily be converted to classification rules. "Why are decision tree classifiers so popular?". The construction of decision tree classifiers does not require any domain knowledge or parameter setting, and therefore is appropriate for exploratory knowledge discovery. Decision trees can handle multi-dimensional data. Their representation of acquired knowledge in tree form is intuitive and generally easy to assimilate by humans. The learning and classification steps of decision tree induction are simple and fast. In general, decision tree classifiers have good accuracy. However, successful use may depend on the data at hand. Decision tree induction algorithms have been used for classification in many application areas such as medicine, manufacturing and production, financial analysis, astronomy, and molecular biology. Decision trees are the basis of several commercial rule induction systems.

Decision Tree Algorithm

During the late 1970s and early 1980s, J. Ross Quinlan, a researcher in machine learning, developed a decision tree algorithm known as ID3 (Iterative Dichotomiser). This work expanded on earlier work on concept learning systems, described by E. B. Hunt, J. Marin, and P.

T. Stone. Quinlan later presented C4.5 (a successor of ID3), which became a benchmark to which newer supervised learning algorithms are often compared. In 1984, a group of statisticians (L. Breiman, J. Friedman, R. Olshen, and C. Stone) published the book Classification and Regression Trees (CART), which described the generation of binary decision trees. ID3 and CART were invented independently of one another at around the same time, yet follow a similar approach for learning decision trees from training tuples. These two cornerstone algorithms spawned a flurry of work on decision tree induction. ID3, C4.5, and CART adopt a greedy (i.e., non backtracking) approach in which decision trees are constructed in a top-down recursive divide-and-conquer manner. Most algorithms for decision tree induction also follow a top-down approach, which starts with a training set of tuples and their associated class labels. The training set is recursively partitioned into smaller subsets as the tree is being built. A basic decision tree algorithm is summarized in Figure 1.1. At first glance, the algorithm may appear long, but fear not! It is quite straightforward. The strategy is as follows. The algorithm is called with three parameters: D, attribute list, and Attribute selection method. D is referred as a data partition. Initially, it is the complete set of training tuples and their associated class labels. The parameter attribute list is a list of attributes describing the tuples. Attribute selection method specifies a heuristic procedure for selecting the attribute that "best" discriminates the given tuples according to class. This procedure employs an attribute selection measure such as information gain or the Gini index. Whether the tree is strictly binary is generally driven by the attribute selection measure. Some attribute selection measures, such as the Gini index, enforce the resulting tree to be binary. Others, like information gain, do not, therein allowing multiway splits (i.e., two or more branches to be grown from a node). The tree starts as a single node, N, representing the training tuples in D (step 1)

Algorithm

Generate decision tree. Generate a decision tree from the training tuples of data partition, D.

Input: Data partition, D, which is a set of training tuples and their associated class labels; attribute list, the set of candidate attributes; Attribute selection method, a procedure to determine the splitting criterion that "best" partitions the data tuples into individual classes. This criterion consists of a splitting attribute and, possibly, either a split-point or splitting subset.

Output: A decision tree.

Step: 1 creates a node N;

Step: 2 if tuples in D are all of the same class, C, then

Step: 3 return N as a leaf node labeled with the class C;

Step: 4 if attribute list is empty then

Step: 5 return N as a leaf node labeled with the majority class in D; // majority voting

Step: 6 apply Attribute selection method (D, attribute list) to find the "best" splitting criterion;

Step: 7 label node N with splitting criterion;

Step: 8 if splitting attribute is discrete-valued and multiway splits allowed then // not restricted to binary trees

Step: 9 attribute list ← attribute list – splitting attribute; // remove splitting attribute

Step: 10 for each outcome j of splitting criterion // partition the tuples and grow subtrees for each partition

Step: 11 let Dj be the set of data tuples in D satisfying outcome j; // a partition

Step: 12 if Dj is empty then

Step: 13 attach a leaf labeled with the majority class in D to node N;

Step: 14 else attach the node returned by Generate decision tree (Dj , attribute list) to node N; end for

Step: 15 return N;

Figure 1.1: Basic Algorithm for Inducing a Decision Tree from Training Tuples

If the tuples in D are all of the same class, then node N becomes a leaf and is labeled with that class (steps 2 and 3). Note that steps 4 and 5 are terminating conditions. All terminating conditions are explained at the end of the algorithm. Otherwise, the algorithm calls Attribute selection method to determine the splitting criterion. The splitting criterion tells us which attribute to test at node N by determining the "best" way to separate or partition the tuples in D into individual classes (step 6). The splitting criterion also tells us which branches to grow from node N with respect to the outcomes of the chosen test. More specifically, the splitting criterion indicates the splitting attribute and may also indicate either a split-point or a splitting subset. The splitting criterion is determined so that, ideally, the resulting partitions at each branch are as "pure" as possible. A partition is pure if all the tuples in it belong to the same class. In other words, if it is split up the tuples in D according to the mutually exclusive outcomes of the splitting criterion, there is a hope for the resulting partitions to be as pure as possible.

Some advantages of decision trees are:

- Simple to understand and interpret. Trees can be visualized.
- Little data preparation required. Other techniques often require data normalization, dummy variables need to be created and blank values to be removed. Note however that this module does not support missing values.
- The cost of using the tree (i.e., predicting data) is logarithmic in the number of data points used to train the tree.
- It can be handled both numerical and categorical data. Other techniques are usually specialized in analyzing datasets that have only one type of variable. See algorithms for more information.
- Multi-output problems are handled.
- A white box model. If a given situation is observable in a model, the explanation for the condition is easily explained by Boolean logic. By contrast, in a black box model (e.g., in an artificial neural network), results may be more difficult to interpret.
- Possible to validate a model using statistical tests. That makes it possible to account for the reliability of the model.
- Performs well even if its assumptions are somewhat violated by the true model from which the data were generated.

The disadvantages of decision trees include:

- Decision-tree learners can create over-complex trees that do not generalize setting the minimum number of samples required at a leaf node or setting the maximum depth of the tree is necessary to avoid this problem.
- Decision trees can be unstable because small variations in the data might result in a completely different tree being generated. This problem is mitigated by using decision trees within an ensemble.
- The problem of learning an optimal decision tree is known to be NP-complete under several aspects of optimality and even for simple concepts. Consequently, practical decision-tree learning algorithms are based on heuristic algorithms such as the greedy algorithm where locally optimal decisions are made at each node. Such algorithms cannot guarantee to return the globally optimal decision tree. This can be mitigated by training multiple trees in an ensemble learner, where the features and samples are randomly sampled with replacement.

- There are concepts that are hard to learn because decision trees do not express them easily, such as XOR, parity or multiplexer problems.

- Decision tree learners create biased trees if some classes dominate and it is therefore recommended to balance the dataset prior to fitting with the decision tree.

Decision Support System

A decision support system (DSS) is a set of expandable, interactive IT techniques and tools designed for processing and analyzing data and for supporting managers in decision making. To do this, the system matches individual resources of managers with computer resources to improve the quality of the decisions made. An exponential increase in operational data has made computers the only tools suitable for providing data for decision-making performed by business managers. This fact has dramatically affected the role of enterprise databases and fostered the introduction of decision support systems. The concept of decision support systems mainly evolved from two research fields: theoretical studies on decision-making processes for organizations and technical research on interactive IT systems. However, the decision support system concept is based on several disciplines, such as databases, artificial intelligence and fuzzy logic, man-machine interaction and simulation.

1.2.2. Sequential Pattern

Data mining consists of extracting information from data stored in databases to understand the data and/or take decisions. Some of the most fundamental data mining tasks are clustering, classification, outlier analysis, and pattern mining. **Pattern mining** consists of discovering interesting, useful, and unexpected patterns in databases Various types of patterns can be discovered in databases such as frequent item sets, associations, sub graphs, sequential rules, and periodic patterns.

The task of **sequential pattern mining** is a data mining task specialized for analyzing **sequential data,** to discover **sequential patterns**. More precisely, it consists of discovering interesting subsequences in **a set of sequences**, where the interestingness of a subsequence can be measured in terms of various criteria such as its occurrence frequency, length, and profit. Sequential pattern mining has numerous real-life applications due to the fact that data is naturally encoded as **sequences of symbols** in many fields such as bioinformatics, e-learning, market basket analysis, texts, and webpage click-stream analysis. Traditionally, **sequential pattern mining** is being used to find sub sequences that appear often in a sequence database, i.e. that are common to several sequences. Those sub sequences are called the **frequent sequential patterns**. For example, in the context of this example, sequential pattern mining can be used to find the sequences of items frequently bought by customers. This can be useful to understand the behaviour of customers to take marketing decisions.

Frequent patterns, as the name suggests, are patterns that occur frequently in data. There are many kinds of frequent patterns, including frequent item sets, frequent sub sequences (also known as sequential patterns), and frequent substructures. A frequent item set typically refers to a set of items that often appear together in a transactional data set for example, milk and bread, which are frequently bought together in grocery stores by many customers. A frequently occurring subsequence, such as the pattern that customers, tend to purchase first a laptop, followed by a digital camera, and then a memory card, is a (frequent) sequential pattern. A substructure can refer to different structural forms (e.g., graphs, trees, or lattices) that may be combined with item sets or sub sequences. If a substructure occurs frequently, it is called a (frequent) structured pattern. Mining frequent patterns leads to the discovery of interesting associations and correlations within data.

1.2.3. Clustering

Clustering is considered as the most important *unsupervised learning* problem; so, as every other problem of this kind, it deals with finding a *structure* in a collection of unlabeled data. A loose definition of clustering could be "the process of organizing objects into groups whose members are similar in some way". A *cluster* is therefore a collection of objects which are "similar" between them and are "dissimilar" to the objects belonging to other clusters. *The Goals of Clustering* so, the goal of clustering is to determine the intrinsic grouping in a set of unlabeled data. But how to decide what constitutes a good clustering? It can be shown that there is no absolute "best" criterion which would be independent of the final aim of the clustering. Consequently, it is the user which must supply this criterion, in such a way that the result of the clustering will suit their needs. For instance, it could be interested in finding representatives for homogeneous groups (*data reduction*), in finding "natural clusters" and describe their unknown properties (*"natural" data types*), in finding useful and suitable groupings (*"useful" data classes*) or in finding unusual data objects (*outlier detection*).

Clustering algorithms can be applied in many fields, for instance:

- *Marketing*: finding groups of customers with similar behavior given a large database of customer data containing their properties and past buying records
- *Biology*: classification of plants and animals given their features
- *Libraries*: book ordering

- *Insurance*: identifying groups of motor insurance policy holders with a high average claim cost; identifying frauds
- *City-planning*: identifying groups of houses according to their house type, value and geographical location
- *Earthquake studies*: clustering observed earthquake epicenters to identify dangerous zones
- *WWW*: document classification; clustering weblog data to discover groups of similar access patterns.

Requirements

The main requirements that a clustering algorithm should satisfy are:
- Scalability
- Dealing with different types of attributes
- Discovering clusters with arbitrary shape
- Minimal requirements for domain knowledge to determine input parameters
- Ability to deal with noise and outliers
- Insensitivity to order of input records
- High dimensionality
- Interpretability and usability.

Classification

Clustering algorithms may be classified as listed below:
- Exclusive Clustering
- Overlapping Clustering
- Hierarchical Clustering
- Probabilistic Clustering

Clustering Algorithm in Identifying Cancerous Data

Clustering algorithm can be used for identifying the cancerous data set. Initially a known samples of cancerous and non cancerous data set is taken for study. Label both the samples data set. Then randomly mix both samples and apply different clustering algorithms into the mixed samples data set (this is known as learning phase of clustering algorithm) and accordingly check the result for how many data set are getting the correct results (since this is known samples which is already know the results beforehand) and hence one can calculate the percentage of correct results obtained. Now, for some arbitrary sample data set if applied on the same algorithm, one can expect the result to be the same percentage correct as one got during the learning phase of the particular algorithm. On this basis one can search for the best suitable clustering algorithm for our data samples. Clustering algorithm can be used in identifying the cancerous data set. Initially one can take known samples of cancerous and non cancerous data set. Label both the samples data set and then randomly mix both samples and apply different clustering algorithms into the mixed samples data set (this is known as learning phase of clustering algorithm) and accordingly check the result for how many data set that are getting the correct results (since this is known samples that are already know the results beforehand) and hence one can calculate the percentage of correct results obtained. Now, for some arbitrary sample data set if one apply the same algorithm he can expect the result to be the same percentage correct as he got during the learning phase of the particular algorithm. On this basis one can search for the best suitable clustering algorithm for the data samples. It has been found through experiment that cancerous data set gives best results with unsupervised non linear clustering algorithms and hence it is concluded the non linear nature of the cancerous data set.

Clustering Algorithm in Search Engines

Clustering algorithm is the backbone behind the search engines. Search engines try to group similar objects in one cluster and the dissimilar objects far from each other. It provides result for the searched data according to the nearest similar object which are clustered around the data to be searched. Better the clustering algorithm used, better are the chances of getting the required result on the front page. Most of the brainstorming activities need to be done for defining the criteria to be used for similar object.

Clustering Algorithm in Academics

It has been found through experiment that cancerous data set gives best results with unsupervised non linear clustering algorithms and hence one can conclude the non linear nature of the cancerous data set.

Clustering Algorithm in Search Engines

Clustering algorithm is the backbone behind the search engines. Search engines try to group similar objects in one cluster and the dissimilar objects far from each other. It provides result for the searched data according to the nearest similar object which are clustered around the data to be searched. Better the clustering algorithm used, better are the chances of getting the required result on the front page. Most of the brainstorming activities need to be done for defining the criteria to be used for similar object.

Clustering Algorithm in Academics

The ability to monitor the progress of students' academic performance has been the critical issue for the academic community of higher learning. Clustering algorithm can be used to monitor the students' academic performance. Based on the students' score they are grouped into different-different clusters (using k-means, fuzzy c-means etc), where each clusters denoting the different level of performance. By knowing the number of students' in each cluster one can know the average performance of a class as a whole.

Clustering Algorithm in Wireless Sensor Network's based Application

Clustering Algorithm can be used effectively in Wireless Sensor Network's based application. One application where it can be used is in Landmine detection. Clustering algorithm plays the role of finding the Cluster heads (or cluster center) which collects all the data in its respective cluster.

1.2.4. Predictive Data Mining

The term Predictive **Data Mining** is usually applied to identify **data mining** projects with the goal to identify a statistical or neural network model or set of models that can be used to **predict** some response of interest.

Here is the criteria for comparing the methods of **Classification and Prediction**– Accuracy – Accuracy of classifier refers to the ability of classifier. It **predicts** the class label correctly and the accuracy of the predictor refers to how well a given predictor can guess the value of predicted attribute for a new **data**.

Prediction Cubes: Prediction Mining in Cube Space

Recently, researchers have turned their attention toward multidimensional data mining to uncover knowledge at varying dimensional combinations and granularities. Such mining is also known as exploratory multidimensional data mining and online analytical data mining (OLAM). Multidimensional data space is huge. In preparing the data, how can one identify the interesting subspaces for exploration? To what granularities should one aggregate the data? Multidimensional data mining in cube space organizes data of interest into intuitive regions at various granularities. It analyzes and mines the data by applying various data mining techniques systematically over these regions. There are at least four ways in which OLAP-style analysis can be fused with data mining techniques:

- Use cube space to define the data space for mining. Each region in cube space represents a subset of data over which one can wish to find interesting patterns. Cube space is defined by a set of expert-designed, informative dimension hierarchies, not just arbitrary subsets of data. Therefore, the use of cube space makes the data space both meaningful and tractable.

- Use OLAP queries to generate features and targets for mining. The features and even the targets (wish to learn to predict) can sometimes be naturally defined as OLAP aggregate queries over regions in cube space.

- Use data mining models as building blocks in a multistep mining process. Multi-dimensional data mining in cube space may consist of multiple steps, where data mining models can be viewed as building blocks that are used to describe the behavior of interesting data sets, rather than the end results.

- Use data cube computation techniques to speed up repeated model construction. Multidimensional data mining in cube space may require building a model for each candidate data space, which is usually too expensive to be feasible. However, by carefully sharing computation across model construction for different candidates based on data cube computation techniques, efficient mining is achievable.

In prediction cubes, an example of multidimensional data mining where the cube space is explored for prediction tasks. A prediction cube is a cube structure that stores prediction models in multidimensional data space and supports prediction in an OLAP manner. Recall that in a data cube, each cell value is an aggregate number (e.g., count) computed over the data subset in that cell. However, each cell value in a prediction cube is computed by evaluating a predictive model built on the data subset in that cell, thereby representing that subset's predictive behaviour. Instead of seeing prediction models as the end result, prediction cubes use prediction models as building blocks to define the interestingness of data subsets, that is, they identify data subsets that indicate more accurate prediction.

1.2.5. Association Rule Mining

Association rule mining is a procedure which is meant to find frequent patterns, correlations, associations, or causal structures from data sets found in various kinds of databases such as relational databases, transactional databases, and other forms of data repositories. Association rules are created by analyzing data for frequent if/then patterns and using the criteria support and confidence to identify the most important relationships. Support is an indication of how frequently the items appear in the database. Confidence indicates the number of times the if/then statements have been found to be true.

In data mining, association rules are useful for analyzing and predicting customer behavior. They play an important part in shopping basket data analysis, product clustering and catalog design and store layout.

Programmers use association rules to build programs capable of machine learning. Machine learning is a type of artificial intelligence (AI) that seeks to build programs with the ability to become more efficient without being explicitly programmed.

- **Minimum support**: The **minimum support** and **minimum** confidence are set by the users, and are parameters of the Apriori algorithm for association rule generation. These parameters are used to exclude rules in the result that have a **support** or a confidence lower than the **minimum support** and **minimum** confidence respectively.

- **Lift value**: The **lift value** is a measure of importance of a **rule**. By using **rule** filters, one can define the desired **lift** range in the settings. The **lift value** of an association **rule** is the **ratio** of the confidence of the **rule** and the expected confidence of the **rule**.

Apriori Algorithm: Apriori uses a "bottom up" approach, where frequent subsets are extended one item at a time (a step **known as** candidate generation), and groups of candidates are tested against the data. The **algorithm** terminates when no further successful extensions are found.

With the quick growth in e-commerce applications, there is an accumulation vast quantity of data in months not in years. Data Mining, also known as Knowledge Discovery in Databases(KDD), to find anomalies, correlations, patterns, and trends to predict outcomes.

Apriori algorithm is a classical algorithm in data mining and it is used for mining frequent itemsets and relevant association rules. It is devised to operate on a database containing a lot of transactions, for instance, items brought by customers in a store. It is very important for effective Market Basket Analysis and it helps the customers in purchasing their items with more ease which increases the sales of the markets. It has also been used in the field of healthcare for the detection of adverse drug reactions. It produces association rules that indicate what all combinations of medications and patient characteristics lead to ADRs.

Association Rules

Association rule learning is a prominent and a well-explored method for determining relations among variables in large databases. Let us take a look at the formal definition of the problem of association rules given by Rakesh Agrawal, the President and Founder of the Data Insights Laboratories.

Let $I = \{i_1, i_2, i_3, ...i_n\}$ be a set of n attributes called items and $D = \{t_1, t_2, ...t_n\}$ be the set of transactions. It is called database. Every transaction, t_i in D has a unique transaction ID, and it consists of a subset of item sets in I. A rule can be defined as an implication, $X \rightarrow Y$ where

X and Y are subsets of I (X, Y $\subseteq$ I,) and they have no element in common, i.e., X ∩ Y, where X and Y are the antecedent and the consequent of the rule, respectively.

Let's take an easy example from the supermarket sphere. The example that are considering is quite small and in practical situations, datasets contain millions or billions of transactions. The set of itemsets, I = {Onion, Burger, Potato, Milk, Beer} and a database consisting of six transactions. Each transaction is a tuple of 0's and 1's where 0 represents the absence of an item and 1 the presence.

Transaction ID	Onion	Potato	Burger	Milk	Beer
t_1	1	1	1	0	0
t_2	0	1	1	1	0
t_3	0	0	0	1	1
t_4	1	1	0	1	0
t_5	1	1	1	0	1
t_6	1	1	1	1	1

An example for a rule in this scenario would be {Onion, Potato}=>{Burger}, which means that if onion and potato are bought, customers also buy a burger.

There are multiple rules possible even from a very small database, so in order to select the interesting ones; constraints are used on various measures of interest and significance and some of these useful measures such as support, confidence, lift and conviction are looked.

Support

The support of an itemset X, **supp(X)** is the proportion of transaction in the database in which the item X appears. It signifies the popularity of an itemset.

Supp(X) =No. of transaction in which X appears/Total number of transactions

In the example above, **supp (Onion)=4/6=0.66667**

If the sales of a particular product (item) above a certain proportion have a meaningful effect on profits, that proportion can be considered as the support threshold. Furthermore, one can identify itemsets that have support values beyond this threshold as significant itemsets.

Confidence

Confidence of a rule is defined as follows:

con f(X➔Y) = supp (X U Y) / supp (X)

It signifies the likelihood of item Y being purchased when item X is purchased. So, for the rule {Onion, Potato} => {Burger}.

This implies that for 75% of the transactions containing onion and potatoes, the rule is correct. It can also be interpreted as the conditional probability **P (Y|X)**, i.e, the probability of finding the itemset Y in transactions given the transaction already contains **X**.

It can give some important insights, but it also has a major drawback. It only takes into account the popularity of the itemset **X** and not the popularity of **Y**. If **Y** is equally popular as **X** then there will be a higher probability that a transaction containing **X** will also contain **Y** thus increasing the confidence. To overcome this drawback there is another measure called lift.

Lift

The lift of a rule is defined as:

$$\text{lift } (X \rightarrow Y) = \text{supp } (X \cup Y) \ / \ (\ \text{supp } (X) * \text{supp } (Y)\ )$$

This signifies the likelihood of the itemset **Y** being purchased when item **X** is purchased while taking into account the popularity of **Y**.

In our example above, If the value of lift is greater than 1, it means that the itemset **Y** is likely to be bought with itemset **X**, while a value less than 1 implies that itemset **Y** is unlikely to be bought if the itemset **X** is bought.

Conviction

The conviction of a rule can be defined as:

$$\text{conv } (X \rightarrow Y) = 1\text{-supp } (Y) \ / \ (\ 1\text{-conf } (X \rightarrow Y)\ )$$

For the rule {onion, potato} => {burger}

The conviction value of 1.32 means that the rule {onion,potato}=>{burger} would be incorrect 32% more often if the association between **X** and **Y** was an accidental chance.

Association rule mining is the data mining process of finding the rules that may govern associations and causal objects between sets of items. So in a given transaction with multiple items, it tries to find the rules that govern how or why such items are often bought together. For example, peanut butter and jelly are often bought together because a lot of people like to make PB&J sandwiches. Also surprisingly, diapers and beer are bought together because, as it turns out, that dads are often tasked to do the shopping while the moms are left with the baby.

The main applications of association rule mining:

- Basket data analysis - is to analyze the association of purchased items in a single basket or single purchase as per the examples given above.

- Cross marketing - is to work with other businesses that complement your own, not competitors. For example, vehicle dealerships and manufacturers have cross marketing campaigns with oil and gas companies for obvious reasons.

- Catalog design - the selection of items in a business' catalog are often designed to complement each other so that buying one item will lead to buying of another. So these items are often complements or very related.

Association rules are created by analyzing data for frequent if/then patterns and using the criteria *support* and *confidence* to identify the most important relationships. *Support* is an indication of how frequently the items appear in the database. *Confidence* indicates the number of times the if/then statements have been found to be true.

In data mining, association rules are useful for analyzing and predicting customer behavior. They play an important part in shopping basket data analysis, product clustering, and catalog design and store layout. Programmers use association rules to build programs capable of machine learning. Machine learning is a type of artificial intelligence (AI) that seeks to build programs with the ability to become more efficient without being explicitly programmed.

1.2.6. *Classification*

Classification is a **data mining** function that assigns items in a collection to target categories or classes. The goal of **classification** is to accurately predict the target class for each case in the **data**. For **example**, a **classification** model could be used to identify loan applicants as low, medium, or high credit risks.

How Does Classification Works?

With the help of the bank loan application that is discussed above, let us understand the working of classification.

The Data Classification process includes two steps:

- Building the Classifier or Model
- Using Classifier for Classification

Building the Classifier or Model

- This step is the learning step or the learning phase.
- In this step the classification algorithms build the classifier.
- The classifier is built from the training set made up of database tuples and their associated class labels.

- Each tuple that constitutes the training set is referred to as a category or class. These tuples can also be referred to as sample, object or data points.

Classification and Prediction Issues

The major issue is preparing the data for Classification and Prediction. Preparing the data involves the following activities:

- **Data Cleaning** – Data cleaning involves removing the noise and treatment of missing values. The noise is removed by applying smoothing techniques and the problem of missing values is solved by replacing a missing value with most commonly occurring value for that attribute.
- **Relevance Analysis** – Database may also have the irrelevant attributes. Correlation analysis is used to know whether any two given attributes are related.
- **Data Transformation and reduction** – The data can be transformed by any of the following methods.
    - **Normalization** – The data is transformed using normalization. Normalization involves scaling all values for given attribute in order to make them fall within a small specified range. Normalization is used when in the learning step, the neural networks or the methods involving measurements are used.
    - **Generalization** – The data can also be transformed by generalizing it to the higher concept. For this purpose one can use the concept hierarchies.

Comparison of Classification and Prediction Methods

Here are the criteria for comparing the methods of Classification and Prediction.

- **Accuracy** – Accuracy of classifier refers to the ability of classifier. It predicts the class label correctly and the accuracy of the predictor refers to how well a given predictor can guess the value of predicted attribute for a new data.
- **Speed** – This refers to the computational cost in generating and using the classifier or predictor.
- **Robustness** – It refers to the ability of classifier or predictor to make correct predictions from given noisy data.
- **Scalability** – Scalability refers to the ability to construct the classifier or predictor efficiently; given large amount of data.
- **Interpretability** – It refers to what extent the classifier or predictor understands.

1.3.   Introduction of Data Warehouse

A data warehouse is a subject-oriented, integrated, time-variant and non-volatile collection of data in support of management's decision making process.

Subject-Oriented: A data warehouse can be used to analyze a particular subject area. For example, "sales" can be a particular subject.

Integrated: A data warehouse integrates data from multiple data sources. For example, source A and source B may have different ways of identifying a product, but in a data warehouse, there will be only a single way of identifying a product.

Time-Variant: Historical data is kept in a data warehouse. For example, one can retrieve data from 3 months, 6 months, 12 months, or even older data from a data warehouse. This contrasts with a transactions system, where often only the most recent data is kept. For example, a transaction system may hold the most recent address of a customer, where a data warehouse can hold all addresses associated with a customer.

Non-volatile: Once data is in the data warehouse, it will not change. So, historical data in a data warehouse should never be altered.

A data warehouse is a copy of transaction data specifically structured for query and analysis.

1.3.1. *Architecture of Data Warehouse*

Data warehouse Architecture is a design that encapsulates all the facets of data warehousing for an enterprise environment. Data warehousing is the creation of a central domain to store complex, decentralized enterprise data in a logical unit that enables data mining, business intelligence, and overall access to all relevant data within an organization. Data warehouse architecture is inclusive of all reporting requirements, data management, security requirements, band width requirements and storage requirements.

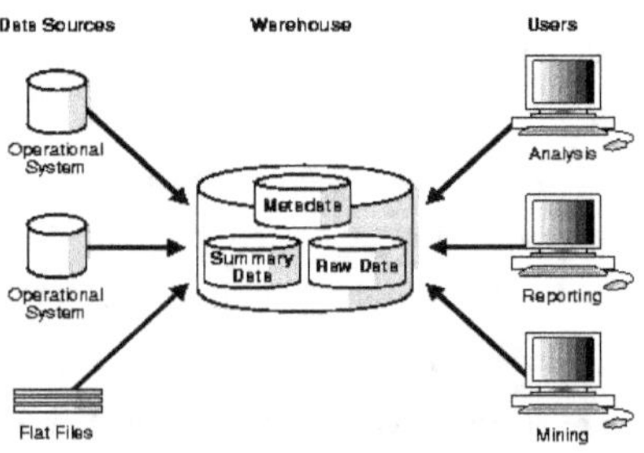

Figure 1.2: Data Warehouse Architecture

Figure 1.2 shows a simple architecture for a data warehouse. End users directly access data derived from several source systems through the data warehouse. In this figure the metadata and raw data of traditional OLTP system is present, as is an additional type of data, summary data. Summaries are very valuable in data warehouses because they pre-compute long operations in advance.The following architecture properties are essential for a data warehouse system [Kelly, 1997]:

- **Separation** Analytical and transactional processing should be kept apart as much as possible.
- **Scalability** Hardware and software architectures should be easy to upgrade as the data volume, which has to be managed and processed, and the number of users' requirements, which have to be met, progressively increase.
- **Extensibility** The architecture should be able to host new applications and technologies without redesigning the whole system.
- **Security** Monitoring accesses is essential because of the strategic data stored in data warehouses.
- **Administerability** Data warehouse management should not be overly difficult.

Single-Layer Architecture

Single-layer architecture is not frequently used in practice. Its goal is to minimize the amount of data stored; to reach this goal, it removes data redundancies. In this case, a data warehouse is virtual. This means that a data warehouse is implemented as a multidimensional view of operational data created by specific middleware, or an intermediate processing layer [Devlin, 1997]. The weakness of this architecture lies in its failure to meet the requirement for separation between analytical and transactional processing. Analysis queries are submitted to operational data after the middleware interprets them. It this way, the queries affect regular transactional workloads. In addition, although this architecture can meet the requirement for integration and correctness of data, it cannot log more data than sources do. For these reasons, a virtual approach to data warehouses can be successful only if analysis needs are particularly restricted and the data volume to analyze is huge.

Two-Layer Architecture

The requirement for separation plays a fundamental role in defining the typical architecture for a data warehouse system. Although it is typically called two-layer architecture to highlight a separation between physically available sources and data warehouses, it actually consists of four subsequent data flow stages [Lechtenbörger, 2001].

- **Source layer:** A data warehouse system uses heterogeneous sources of data. That data is originally stored to corporate relational databases or legacy1 databases, or it may come from information systems outside the corporate walls.

- **Data staging:** The data stored to sources should be extracted, cleansed to remove inconsistencies and fill gaps, and integrated to merge heterogeneous sources into one common schema. The so-called Extraction, Transformation, and Loading tools (ETL) can merge heterogeneous schemata, extract, transform, cleanse, validate, filter, and load source data into a data warehouse [Jarke et al., 2000]. Technologically speaking, this stage deals with problems that are typical for distributed information systems, such as inconsistent data management and incompatible data structures [Zhuge et al., 1996].

- **Data warehouse layer:** Information is stored to one logically centralized single repository: a data warehouse. The data warehouse can be directly accessed, but it can also be used as a source for creating data marts, which partially replicate data warehouse contents and are designed for specific enterprise departments. Meta-data repositories store information on sources, access procedures, data staging, users, data mart schemata, and so on.

- **Analysis:** In this layer, integrated data is efficiently and flexibly accessed to issue reports, dynamically analyze information and simulate hypothetical business scenarios. Technologically speaking, it should feature aggregate data navigators, complex query optimizers, and user-friendly GUIs.

The architectural difference between data warehouses and data marts needs to be studied closer. It acts as a centralized storage system for all the data being summed up.

Data marts can be viewed as small, local data warehouses replicating (and summing up as much as possible) the part of a primary data warehouse required for a specific application domain.

Cleaning Operation: Clean and process the operational data before putting it into the warehouse and do this programmatically, although most data warehouses use a staging area instead. A staging area simplifies building summaries and general warehouse management.

Data Staging Area: A place where data is processed before entering the warehouse. Data staging area is where the raw operational data is extracted, cleaned, transformed and combined so that it can be reported on and queried by users. This area lies between the operational source systems and the user database and is typically not accessible to users.

Data Mart: Data mart is a logical subset of an enterprise-wide data warehouse. For example, a data warehouse for a retail chain is constructed incrementally from individual, conformed data marts dealing with separate subject areas such as product sales. Dimensional Data marts are organized by subject area such as sales, finance and marketing and coordinated data category such as customer, product and location. These flexible information stores allows data structures to respond to business changes-product line additions, new staff, responsibilities, mergers, consolidations, and acquisitions.

1.3.2. *Applications of Data Warehouse*

Data warehouses and data marts are used in a wide range of applications. Business executives use the data in data warehouses and data marts to perform data analysis and make strategic decisions. In many firms, data warehouses are used as an integral part of a *plan-execute-assess* "closed-loop" feedback system for enterprise management. Data warehouses are used extensively in banking and financial services, consumer goods and retail distribution sectors, and controlled manufacturing, such as demand based production.

Typically, the longer a data warehouse has been in use, the more it will have evolved. This evolution takes place throughout a number of phases. Initially, the data warehouse is mainly used for generating reports and answering predefined queries. Progressively, it is used to analyze summarized and detailed data, where the results are presented in the form of reports and charts. Later, the data warehouse is used for strategic purposes, performing multidimensional analysis and sophisticated slice-and-dice operations. Finally, the data warehouse may be employed for knowledge discovery and strategic decision making using data mining tools. In this context, the tools for data warehousing can be categorized into *access and retrieval tools, database reporting tools, data analysis tools*, and *data mining tools*. Business users need to have the means to know what exists in the data warehouse (through metadata), how to access the contents of the data warehouse, how to examine the contents using analysis tools, and how to present the results of such analysis.

There are three kinds of data warehouse applications: *information processing, analytical processing*, and *data mining*: Information processing supports querying, basic statistical analysis, and reporting using crosstabs, tables, charts, or graphs. A current trend in data warehouse information processing is to construct low-cost Web-based accessing tools that are then integrated with Web browsers. Analytical processing supports basic OLAP operations, including slice-and-dice, drill-down, roll-up, and pivoting. It generally operates on historical data in both summarized and detailed forms. The major strength of on-line analytical processing over information processing is the multidimensional data analysis of data warehouse data. Data mining supports knowledge discovery by finding hidden patterns and associations, constructing analytical models, performing classification and prediction and presenting the mining results using visualization tools.

Summary

Various types of data mining techniques such as Decision Trees, Sequential Pattern, Clustering, Predictive Data Mining, Association Rule Mining, Classification algorithms have been discussed in this chapter. Each and every component of data mining system has its own role and importance in completing data mining efficiently. These different modules need to interact correctly with each other in order to complete the complex process of data mining successfully. Finally, the basics of data warehouse, various architectural styles and its applications are presented.

Review Questions

1. What is data mining? Write down the properties of data mining.
2. Briefly discuss about the Data Mining Techniques.
3. Write in short about Decision Trees.
4. Briefly describe about Sequential Pattern.
5. Give a short account on clustering algorithm in various fields.
6. Illustrate about Predictive Data Mining.
7. Discuss about Association Rule mining in detail.
8. How Does Classification Works?
9. Define data warehouse and describe the architecture of data warehouse.

CHAPTER 2

INFORMATION RETRIEVAL AND KNOWLEDGE DISCOVERY

2.1.   Introduction

Information retrieval (**IR**) is the activity of obtaining information resources relevant to an information need from a collection of information resources. Searches can be based on full-text or other content-based indexing. Information retrieval is the science of searching for information in a document, searching for documents themselves, and also searching for metadata that describe data, and for databases of texts, images or sounds. Information retrieval, the techniques of storing and recovering and often disseminating recorded data especially through the use of a computerized system.

The information retrieval research states that there are no proper well-established methods for the information search. An Interactive Information Retrieval (IIR) system should be established to make this process easy and simple. The study about interactive information retrieval system gives an idea that interaction must be between the user and system as well as the user and the information. To obtain a success, it would extract the content which is related to the user query. Information retrieval is learned by various fields such as psychology, human–computer interaction, information and library science and traditional Information Retrieval (IR).Ian Ruthven et al., [2007] stated that human computer information retrieval is similar to the interactive information retrieval.

According to Salton [1992], the user endeavour procedures are significant components of Information retrieval evaluation, including the attitudes and perceptions of users. The review of IR system evaluation along with its methodologies and methods are discussed by [P. Cowley, 2006; F. Crestani, 2006 and R. Capra, 2006]. The traditional information retrieval methods do not fit perfectly with IIR study situations but they lead a way for study of design and measurement. Taking the context of IIR evaluations, baselines [Diane Kelly, 2009] are often considered as a substitute to the experimental system.

The baseline is more often correspond to one level of the incentive variable. A baseline is one of the traditional models which is nothing but a status quo that raises some appealing query with respect to IIR evaluations and in most cases, it would be a commercial search engine.

Search engine is a prominent solution for the user to retrieve the appropriate information based on their needs and the search engines like Google, Yahoo, etc., are the familiar search engines used by ample range of peoples. The main core of these applications was information retrieval which is an extremely hefty process within Natural Language Processing (NLP). Even though various applications are in this information retrieval, the text clustering took the major part. In text clustering, set of texts on some groups are grouped based on some common relationship. It makes the search engine in an effectual manner for information retrieval within a short time. The main objective of NLP is the retrieved information that gathers meaningful information from large database. The difficulty is the structure of database because data should be in various kinds such as unstructured, amorphous which are difficult to deal.

Commonly, a well-organized management system for huge collections of text is a difficult problem in practice. The increasing technology and development in the use of network services and text collections such as digital libraries are quite increased and distributed. The queries are in the contrast to Boolean queries, which has no precise set of documents that constitute the answers and there is no proper mechanism for recognizing the documents that should be returned for the user query. The recent issue is to the Boolean queries, there is no accurate set of documents that constitute the relative answers for the user query and no proper mechanism for identifying which documents should be returned as the result for the user query. The data transmission and unnecessary access to sub-collections are the major problems that must be addressed in construction of a practical system for information retrieval. "Reliability and Validity" are considered as the most central issue in IR evaluation, especially in the current situation where there is mounting conversation in the research community about reproducibility and generalizability of the results. The information is to be accessed and used which requires explicit functionalities that go beyond the uncomplicated search interaction. This circumstance often plays a vital role and that should be considered for the information system. There is a lack of appropriate evaluation methods for considering contexts and new functions.

2.2.   Knowledge Discovery in Database

With the enormous amount of data stored in files, databases and other repositories, it is increasingly important to develop powerful means for analysis and perhaps interpretation of such data for the extraction of interesting knowledge that could help in decision-making. Data Mining, also popularly known as Knowledge Discovery in Databases (KDD), refers to as "*the nontrivial process of identifying valid, novel, potentially useful and ultimately understandable pattern in data*". While data mining and knowledge discovery in databases are frequently treated as synonyms, data mining is actually a part of the knowledge discovery process. Figure 2.1 shows that data mining as a step in an iterative knowledge discovery process. The task of the knowledge discovery and data mining process is to extract knowledge from data such that the resulting knowledge is useful in a given application.

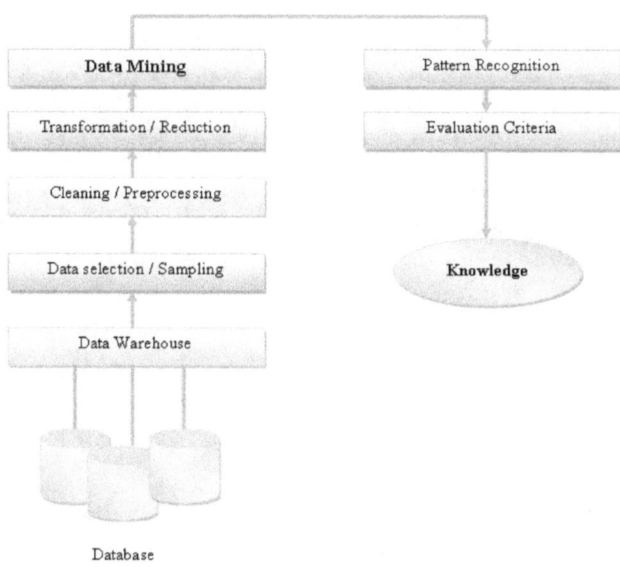

Figure 2.1: Complete Overview of Knowledge Discovery from Databases

The Knowledge Discovery process in Databases comprises of a few steps leading from raw data collections to some form of retrieving new knowledge. The iterative process consists of the following steps:

- **Data cleaning:** Also known as data cleansing, it is a phase in which noisy and irrelevant data are removed from the collection.
- **Data integration:** At this stage, multiple data sources, often heterogeneous, may be combined in a common source.
- **Data selection:** At this step, the data which is relevant to the analysis is decided on and retrieved from the data collection.
- **Data mining:** It is the crucial step in which clever techniques are applied to extract data patterns which is potentially useful.

- **Pattern evaluation:** In this step, strictly interesting patterns representing Knowledge is identified which is based on given measures.

- **Knowledge representation:** Is the final phase in which the discovered knowledge is visually represented to the user. This essential step uses visualization techniques to help users to understand and interpret the data mining results.

It is common practice to combine some of these steps together for specific application. For instance, data cleaning and data integration can be performed together as a pre-processing phase to generate a data warehouse. Data selection and data transformation can also be combined where the consolidation of the data is the result of the selection or as for the case of data warehouses, the selection is done on transformed data and the KDD is an iterative process. Once the discovered knowledge is presented to the user, the evaluation measures can be enhanced and the mining can be further refined and new data can be selected or further transformed or new data sources can be integrated in order to get different and more appropriate results.

Three Types of Information Systems

Information-Retrieval Systems (IR): Search large bodies of information which are not specifically formatted as formal data bases, Web search engine, and Keyword search of a text base, typically read-only.

Database Management Systems (DBMS): Relatively small schema, large body of homogeneous data, Minor or no deductive capability, Extensive formal update capability, Shared use for both read and write.

Knowledge-Base Systems (KBS): Relatively small body of heterogeneous information, significant deductive capability and support of an intelligent application.

2.3. Data Mining Models

There are several data mining models. Some of these models are narrated below which are conceived to be important in the area of "Data Mining" [N. Ye, 2003; J. Han and M. Kamber, 2006].

Clustering: It segments a large set of data into subsets or clusters. Each cluster is a collection of data objects that are similar to one another with the same cluster but dissimilar to object in other clusters [N. Ye, 2003; J. Han and M. Kamber, 2006; R. Dubes and A. Jain, 1998; A. K. Jain et al., 1999; L. Kaufman and P. J. Rousseeuw, 1990].

Classification: Decision trees, also known as classification trees, are a statistical tool that partitions a set of records into disjunctive classes. The records are given as tuples with several numerics and categorical attributes with one additional attribute being the class to predict. Decision trees algorithm differs in selection of variables to split and how they pick the splitting point [N. Ye, 2003; J. Han and M. Kamber, 2006].

Association Mining: It uncovers interesting correlation patterns among a large set of data items by showing attribute value conditions that occur together frequently [N. Ye, 2003; J. Han and M. Kamber, 2006].

2.3.1. *Clustering*

The process of grouping a set of objects into classes of similar objects is called clustering and a cluster is a collection of data objects that are similar to one another within the same cluster and are dissimilar to the objects in other clusters. A cluster of data objects can be treated collectively as one group and so may be considered as a form of data compression. Although classification is an effective means for distinguishing groups or classes of objects, it is often more desirable to proceed in the reverse direction: First, partition the set of data into groups based on data similarity (e.g., using clustering) and then assign labels to the relatively small number of groups. Additional advantage of such a clustering- based process is that it is adaptable to changes and helps to single out useful features that distinguish different groups.

Clustering is also called as data segmentation in some applications because clustering partitions large data sets into groups according to their similarity. As a data mining function, cluster analysis can be used as a stand-alone tool to gain insight into the distribution of data, to observe the characteristics of each cluster and to focus on a particular set of clusters for further analysis. Alternatively, it may serve as a pre-processing step for various algorithms, such as characterization, attribute subset selection and classification which would then operate on the detected clusters and the selected attributes or features.

Data clustering is under vigorous development and contributing areas of research include data mining, statistics, machine learning, spatial database technology and marketing. Owing to the huge amounts of data collected in databases, cluster analysis has recently become a highly active topic in data mining research. Clustering techniques are considered as efficient tools for partitioning data sets in order to get homogeneous clusters of objects and these techniques [A.K.Jain and R.C.Dubes, 1988] are among the well-known machine learning techniques. Clustering techniques are widely used in many domains such as medicine, banking, finance, marketing, security, etc. They work under an unsupervised mode when the class label of each object in the training set is not known.

Clustering is the state of grouping of set of text together in the same groups which are similar to each other. Cluster analysis is the collection of patterns based on similarity. The main work of clustering is discovering a structure in a collection of unlabelled data. Simple words are "similar" between them and are "dissimilar" to the objects belonging to other clusters. Generally the term "clustering" is used by several research communities in the motto grouping unlabelled data. There were multiple terminologies and assumptions for clustering. The major drawback is not to find the common clustering technique which was applicable universally in order to cover the variety of structures present in multi-dimensional data sets. The objective of clustering is useful to systematize the documents which will improve the process of retrieval and support browsing [Peter G. Anick and ShivakumarVaithyanathan, 1997; Piroui et al., 1996]. The formal methods are intensively keen in the case of quantitative data [SudiptoGuha et al., 1998].

Clustering is naturally an unsupervised learning method which can be leveraged to increase the effectiveness of the results and it is a supervised variant. In particular, word-clusters and co-training methods can be used in order to improve the accuracy of a classification by supervised applications with the use of clustering techniques. The text document can be symbolized in the form of binary data when using the presence or absence of a word in the document in order to create a binary vector. In such cases, it is possible to directly use a variety of categorical data clustering algorithms [Periklis Andritsos, 2004] on the binary representation. In clustering, the frequency is a term to avoid the unwanted dominating effect of any single term that might be very frequent in a document.

Clustering reduces the significance of general terms in the data collection; make certain things matching of documents which would be influenced by that of more discriminative words which have relatively low frequencies in the data collection. The benefit of clustering is useful for grouping, decision making, pattern analysis and machine learning. In addition to data mining, image segmentation along with document retrieval only few prior information are available about the data according to the user query. The decision maker must have some assumptions about the extracted data that may be possible but the accuracy is not acquired. These restrictions make the clustering terminology appropriate to inter-relationships among the data points of their structure.

Components of a Clustering Task

- Typical pattern clustering activity involves the following steps [Jain and Dubes 1988].
- Pattern representation (optionally including feature extraction or selection)
- Definition of a pattern proximity measure appropriate to the data domain
- Clustering or grouping
- Data abstraction (if needed) and
- Assessment of output (if needed).

Figure 2.2 depicts a typical sequencing of the first three of these steps, including a feedback path where the grouping process output could affect subsequent feature extraction and similarity computations. Pattern representation refers to the number of classes, the number of available patterns, the number, type and scale of the features available to the clustering algorithm. Feature selection is the process of identifying the most effective subset of the original features to use in clustering. Feature extraction is the use of one or more transformations of the input features to produce new salient features. Either or both of these techniques can be used to obtain an appropriate set of features to use in clustering. Pattern proximity is usually measured by a distance function defined on pairs of patterns. A variety of distance measures are used in the various communities [Anderberg 1973; Jain and Dubes 1988; Diday and Simon 1976]. A simple distance measure like Euclidean distance can often be used to reflect dissimilarity between two patterns, whereas other similarity measures can be used to characterize the conceptual similarity between patterns

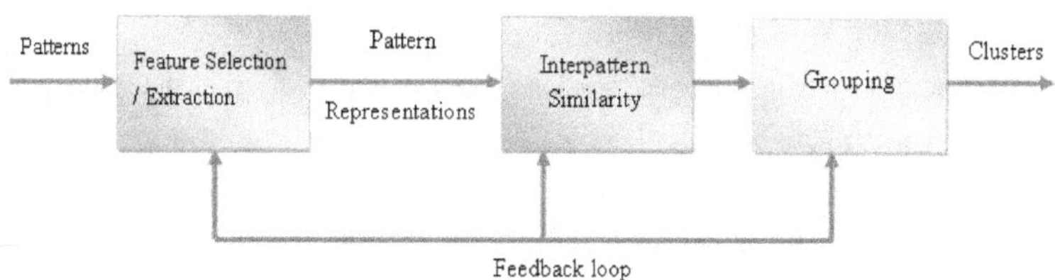

Figure 2.2: Stages in Clustering [Michalski and Stepp 1983]

The grouping step can be performed in a number of ways. The output clustering can be hard (a partition of the data into groups) or fuzzy (where each pattern has a variable degree of membership in each of the output clusters). Hierarchical clustering algorithms produce a nested series of partitions based on a criterion for merging or splitting clusters based on similarity. Partitional clustering algorithms identify the partition that optimizes (usually locally) a clustering criterion. Additional techniques for the grouping operation include probabilistic [Brailovski 1991] and graph-theoretic [Zahn 1971] clustering methods.

Data abstraction is the process of extracting a simple and compact representation of a data set. Simplicity is either from the perspective of automatic analysis (so that a machine can perform further processing efficiently) or from human-oriented approach (so that the representation obtained is easy to comprehend and intuitively appealing). In the clustering context, a typical data abstraction is a compact description of each cluster, usually in terms of cluster prototypes or representative patterns such as the centroid [Diday and Simon 1976].

2.3.2. Classification

Huge amount of data is being collected and stored in databases from various sources which would also increase period by period. The major problem is the invaluable information and knowledge "hidden" on those databases and it is totally impossible to mine them without a proper automatic extracting method.

In recent years, various algorithms were created to extract which is called nuggets of knowledge from huge database.

- Predicts categorical class labels
- Classifies data (constructs a model) based on the training set and the values(class labels) in a classifying attribute and uses it in classifying new data.

Classification is a two-step process which comprises of:

Model construction: describing a set of pre-determined classes

- Each tuple/sample is assumed to belong to a pre-defined class, as determined by the class label attribute
- The set of tuples used for model construction. For example, training set.
- The model is represented as classification rules, decision trees or mathematical formulae.

Model usage: for classifying future or unknown objects

- Estimate accuracy of the model
- The known label of test sample is compared with the classified result from the model
- Accuracy rate is the percentage of test set samples that are correctly classified by the model
- Test set is independent of training set, otherwise over-fitting will occur

There are two types of Classifications namely supervised and unsupervised and these classifications are discussed below:

Supervised Classification

The training data (observations, measurements, etc.) are accompanied by labels indicating the class of the observations. New data is classified based on the training set. The set of possible classes is well-known in advance. The input data, also called the training set consists of multiple records each having multiple attributes or features. This model is used to classify test data for which the class descriptions are not known. The characteristics of this type are:

- Each record is tagged with a class label.
- The objective of classification is to analyze the input data and to develop an accurate description or model for each class using the features present in the data.

Unsupervised Classification

Classification is nothing but a result prediction based on a given input and to progress this approach, a training set containing a set of attributes and the respective outcome, usually called as prediction attribute. The set of possible classes is not known in this category, after assigning a name to that class. The result prediction is based on the relationships between the attributes. The prediction set is nothing but a result which was not seen before. An efficient algorithm defines how the accuracy of the prediction can be obtained. The below dataset illustrates the prediction which is generally based on the medical dataset.

Most of the prediction rules are generally based on IF conditions. IF part consists of a conjunction of conditions and the rule consequent THEN part certainly a rule predicting the first row in the training set. The prediction rule stated above can be represented by

IF (Age = 65 AND Heart rate > 70) OR (Age > 60 AND Blood pressure > 140/70) THEN Heart problem = yes (Table 2.1 and Table 2.2)

Based on the above rule, pleasing any of these smaller rules means that the consequent is the prediction.

2.3.3. Associate Mining in Database

Association rules are most popular among the researchers in discovering the relations between variables in large databases. Association rules are commonly used for data exploration and description. The researchers use these mining rules mainly for the purpose of prediction that is more popular among the data mining community [Rudin et al., 2011; Takashi

Washio et al., 1998]. The well-known association rule in mining algorithm is Apriori that requires item list and its limits for the prediction. The rules are used for the creation of item list which enables the construction of item sets based on their supersets which will form valid rules. Thus, progress of the time performance of an item set construction performs in an effective manner.

The objective of association rules is to avoid long mining times which can produce a large compilation of rules with low projecting power. The reason behind the popularity of association rules are the descriptive nature and easily understandable representation [Rakesh Agrawal et al., 1993]. The challenges to be faced in using the associate rules are generating an appropriate number of rules that can be useful in developing predictive models. Most of the association rules coordinate with the classifications [Weiyang Lin et al., 2000] and the best example of association rule is WEKA. The classification association rules are generated by using Apriori Sets and Sequences algorithm [Keith A. Pray, 2004]. These associate rules provide an efficient way for providing the associative patterns from market basket data.

<table>
<tr><td colspan="4" align="center">Table 2.1: Training Medical Data Set</td><td colspan="4" align="center">Table 2.2: Prediction Set</td></tr>
<tr><td>Age</td><td>Heart Rate</td><td>Blood Pressure</td><td>Heart Problem</td><td>Age</td><td>Heart Rate</td><td>Blood Pressure</td><td>Heart Problem</td></tr>
<tr><td>65</td><td>78</td><td>150/70</td><td>Yes</td><td>43</td><td>98</td><td>147/89</td><td>?</td></tr>
<tr><td>37</td><td>83</td><td>112/76</td><td>No</td><td>65</td><td>58</td><td>106/63</td><td>?</td></tr>
<tr><td>71</td><td>67</td><td>108/65</td><td>No</td><td>84</td><td>77</td><td>150/65</td><td>?</td></tr>
</table>

Table 2.3: A Small Database for Associate Mining

ID	MILK	BREAD	BUTTER	BEER
1	1	1	0	0
2	0	0	1	0
3	0	0	0	1
4	1	1	1	0
5	0	1	0	0

The intention is to analyse data to identify the patterns associating different attributes from that data set. The common problem in association mining rule is the lack of confidence that arises due to the transactions. In a set of items assume a least threshold and a least confidence threshold the rules that satisfy in the data specified the support and confidence threshold but the frequency of the measures is not efficient. In the table 2.3 the set of items are I= {MILK, BREAD, BUTTER, BEER} in which {BUTTER, BREAD} => {MILK}, i.e., if the customer buy butter and bread then the customer will also buy milk [Agrawal, R, 1993].

In Figure 2.3, frequent itemset lattice, where the color of the box indicates how many transactions contain the combination of items. The lower levels of the lattice can contain at most the minimum number of their parents' items; e.g. {ac} can have only at most items and this is called the downward-closure property. The problem is in a large dataset downward-closure property generates too many items that turn out not to have minimum support, causing it to waste of too much effort. This wastage decreases dramatically from the third pass onwards. The word (ID) is to store an item rather than requiring as many words as the number of items in the dataset. It is effective when the size of dataset becomes small compared to the huge size of the database. If datasets can fit in memory and the distribution of the frequent item sets has an end but it doesn't fit in memory, then there is a jump in the execution time.

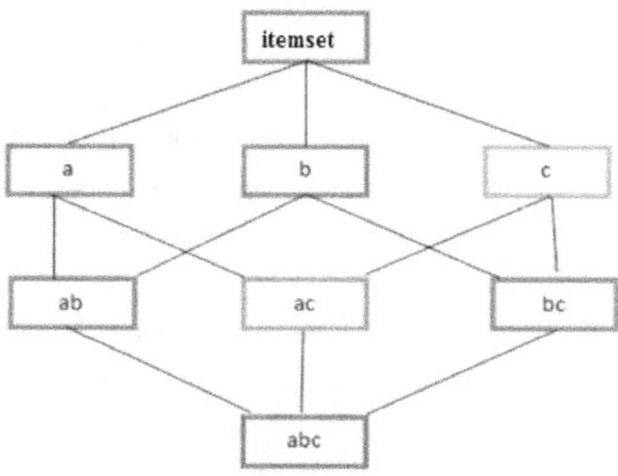

Figure 2.3: Frequent Itemset

Mining Complexity

Association mining works as follows. Let I be a set of items and D a database of transactions where each transaction has a unique identifier (tid) and contains a set of items called an itemset. An itemset with k items is called a k -itemset. The support of an itemset X, denoted σ (X) is the number of transactions in which that itemset occurs as a subset. A k-subset is a k - length subset of an itemset. An itemset is frequent or large if its support is more than a user-specified minimum support (min_sup) value. F_k is the set of frequent k–itemsets and as frequent itemset is maximal if it is not a subset of any other frequent itemset.

2.4. Clustering

The clustering is introduced in order to find the word which captures most of the information about the document that is similar. The art of clustering can be treated as an optimization problem by finding a small number of classes with low intra-class alteration or with high intra-class connectivity. The difficulty is the distance or distortion measures because it may not accurately show the structure of the different mechanism in the high dimensional data.

Data Types

As well-known data mining is the concept of mining a relative data from a huge database at the same time in a meaningful manner. The important issue is what kind of data to be mined. Since the data is stored in various types such as warehouse data, database data and transactional data. The problem of choosing the kind the data to be mined is an interesting area of research. This shows that various types of data and information repositories on which the data mining can be performed. In general, database that has the set of records in which each individual is characterized by a set of attributes. The domain has those attributes which takes the values of the attributes is called as simple value or attribute values. If more numbers of attributes are added in a record then those are in order list which are otherwise called as tuples.

In the process clustering, the analysis is based on the data in the tuple such as persons, salaries, opinions, software entities and many others. These datasets are for identifying the differences among data elements. There are two types of database namely vertical and horizontal database. In case of vertical database, each label is associated with its corresponding Object Identifier (OID) list, the set of all OIDs where it appears. In the horizontal database, each object has an OID along with the sequence of item sets comprising the object. Comparing these two types, vertical database is more effective. The reason is that the vertical format narrows the data only to the subset. The major problem of Vertical database type approach is related to the number of connections that is essential to perform and to estimate the support of large item sets. Specific optimizations are required for the reduction of intersections.

Classification based on Size

Clustering classification is more important issue in the problem of categorical data clustering because it classifies the data objects based on the size of their domain and the number of distinct values of the data objects. Consider a database D of n objects. If x', y', z' are the three objects in the database D, each one has $x'=(x_1,x_2,......x_m)$, $y'=(y_1,y_2,.....y_m)$ and $z'=(z_1,z_2,......z_m)$, where m is the dimensionality while each individual x_i, y_i, and z_i, $1<i<m$, is the feature or the object of the corresponding attribute. These attributes work on two conditions, i.e. *continuous if and discrete if.* An attribute is *continuous if* two values of attributes exists an infinite value. In case of *discrete if*, its domain is into a one-to-one correspondence with a finite subset of the positive integers. In *discrete if* process attributes are according to the measurement scales. Scale is nothing but a way of ordering the data and thus, a way to compare the values of a particular domain. Scale follows the following classes:

In a nominal scale that is $x_i = y_i$, $x_i \neq y_i$, it cannot be totally ordered.

In an ordinal scale, the additional features' values can be totally ordered but the thing is that the scale points cannot be quantified.

$$x_i = y_i, \text{ or } x_i < y_i \text{ or } x_i > y_i.$$

An interval scale can tell not only if one value comes before or after another but also how far before or after. Not only $x_i > y_i$ but also the $x_i - y_i$.

A ratio scale is interval scales with the meaningful zero point, i.e. the zero point ratio values are x_i/y_i which is meaningful.

Concept of Similarity and Dissimilarity

Similarity measure is defined as the similarity between two patterns drawn from the same feature spaces which are required for most clustering procedures. The distance measure is chosen carefully, at the same time the dissimilarity is among the two patterns using distance on the feature space. The similarity is calculated by computing similarity ij^{th} entry gives the similarity between the ith and ji^{th} clusters. By combing the closets of two clusters, the similarity matrix is updated regularly for pair wise similarity between the original cluster and the new one. Goodness or a quality is measured by the best entropy which is obtained when each cluster contains exactly one data point. The intension is to find a proper way to decide how far or how close the data objects are from one another. This similarity or dissimilarity is most helpful in the process of classification.

If the coordination between the two objects are larger, their similarity is large and if the coordination is small, the similarity is also small and there exists variety of distance measure in the literature [Anderberg 1973; Jain and Dubes 1988; Diday and Simon 1976].The distance can be measured by using any one of a variety of distance measures in which those measures depend on the type of attributes.

Let three data objects x', y', z' all these are D in database.

$d(x', y') \geq 0$: non $-$ negativity;

$d(x', y') = 0$ if and only if $x' = y'$: identity;

$d(x', y') = d(y', x')$: symmetry;

$d(x', z') \leq d(x', y') + d(y', z')$: triangle inequality;

The in this distance of objects x' and y';

$$d(x', y') = \left(\sum_{i=1}^{m} |x_i - y_i|q\right)^{1/q}$$

Where q is the positive integer,

For q=2,

Then, $d(x', y') = \sqrt{\sum_{i=1}^{m}(x_i - y_i)^2}$

For q=1;

Then, $d(x', y') = d(x', y') = \sum_{i=1}^{m} |x_i - y_i|$

For $q \to \infty$, the maximum distance is expressed as,

$$d(x', y') = max_{i=1}^{m} |x_i - y_i|.$$

Text Clustering

The objective of clustering is to partition an unstructured set of objects into clusters and one often wants the objects to be as similar to objects in the same cluster and as dissimilar to objects from other clusters as possible. Clustering has been used in many different areas and there exists a multitude of different clustering algorithms for different settings [Jain et al., 1999]. A clustering algorithm finds a partition of a set of objects that fulfils some criterion based on these conditions. To use most clustering algorithms two components are necessary:

- an object representation,
- a similarity (or distance) measure between objects.

Clustering is an unsupervised learning method and the result (the clustering, the partition) is based solely on the object representation i.e. the similarity measure and the clustering algorithm. If these correspond to the users' understanding of the result that might well be an intuitive and useful clustering. Though, one must keep in mind that clustering algorithms always produce clustering, even when this is not justified and that there in most cases, exist many relevant clustering of a set of complex objects.

The problem of clustering finds applicability for a number of tasks:

- **Document Organization and Browsing**: The hierarchical organization of documents into coherent categories can be very useful for systematic browsing of the document collection. A classical example of this is the Scatter/Gather method [D. Cutting, 1992], which provides a systematic browsing technique with the use of clustered organization of the document collection.

- **Corpus Summarization:** Clustering techniques provide a coherent summary of the collection in the form of cluster-digests [H. Schutze and C. Silverstein, 1997] or word-clusters [L. Baker, 1998; R. Bekkerman et al., 2001], which can be used in order to provide summary insights into the overall content of the underlying corpus. Variants of such methods, especially sentence clustering, can also be used for document summarization. The problem of clustering is also closely related to that of dimensionality reduction and topic modelling. Such dimensionality reduction methods are all deferent ways of summarizing a corpus of documents.

- **Document Classification**: While clustering is inherently an un-supervised learning method, it can be leveraged in order to improve the quality of the results in its supervised variant. In particular, word-clusters [L. Baker, 1998; R. Bekkerman et al., 2001] and co-training methods [K. Nigam, 1998] can be used in order to improve the classification accuracy of supervised applications with the use of clustering techniques.

In many classes of algorithms such as the k-means algorithm, hierarchical algorithms or general-purpose methods which can be extended to any kind of data, including text data. A text document can be represented either in the form of binary data in the presence or absence of a word in the document in order to create a binary vector. In such cases, it is possible to directly use a variety of categorical data clustering algorithms [P. Andritsos et al., 2004; D. Gibson et al., 1998; S. Guha et al., 1999] on the binary representation. A more enhanced representation would include refined weighting methods based on the frequencies of the individual words in the document as well as frequencies of words in an entire collection (e.g., Term Frequency – Inverse Document Frequency (TF-IDF) weighting [G. Salton and C. Buckley, 1988]). Quantitative data clustering algorithms [S. Guha et al., 1999; R. Ng and J. Han, 1994; T. Zhang et al., 1996] can be used in conjunction, with these frequencies, in order to determine the most relevant groups of objects in the data.

However, such naive techniques do not typically work well for clustering text data. This is because text data has a number of unique properties which necessitate the design of specialized algorithms for the task. The distinguishing characteristics of the text representation are as follows:

The dimensionality of the text representation is very large but the underlying data is sparse. In other words, the lexicon from which the documents are drawn may be of the order of 10^5, but a given document may contain only a few hundred words. This problem is even more serious when the documents to be clustered are very short (e.g., when clustering sentences or tweets).While the lexicon of a given corpus of documents may be large, the words are typically correlated with one another. This means that the number of concepts (or principal components) in the data is much smaller than the feature space. This necessitates the careful design of algorithms which can account for word correlations in the clustering process. The number of words (or non-zero entries) in the different documents may vary widely. Therefore, it is important to normalize the document representations appropriately during the clustering task.

The sparse and high dimensional representation of the different documents necessitate the design of text-specific algorithms for document representation and processing which is a topic heavily studied in the information retrieval literature where many techniques have been proposed to optimize document representation for improving the accuracy of matching a document with a query [G. Salton & C. Buckley, 1988; R.A. Baeza-Yates and B.A. Ribeiro-Neto, 2011]. Most of these techniques can also be used to improve document representation for clustering.

Feature Selection and Transformation Methods for Text Clustering

The quality of any data mining method such as classification and clustering is highly dependent on the noisiness of the features that are used for the clustering process. For example, commonly used words such as "the", may not be very useful in improving the clustering quality. Therefore, it is critical to select the features effectively, so that the noisy words in the corpus are removed before the clustering. In addition to feature selection, a number of feature transformation methods such as Latent Semantic Indexing (LSI), Probabilistic Latent Semantic Analysis (PLSA) and Non-negative Matrix Factorization (NMF) are available to improve the quality of the document representation and make it more amenable to clustering. In these techniques (often called dimension reduction), the correlations among the words in the lexicon are leveraged in order to create features, which correspond to the concepts or principal components in the data.

Feature Selection Methods: Feature selection is more common and easy technique to apply in the problem of text categorization [Y. Yang, J. O. Pederson., 1995] in which supervision is available for the feature selection process. However, a number of simple unsupervised methods can also be used for feature selection in text clustering. Some examples of such methods are discussed below.

Document Frequency-based Selection: The simplest possible method for feature selection in document clustering is that of the use of document frequency to filter out irrelevant features. While the use of inverse document frequencies reduces the importance of such words, this may not alone be sufficient to reduce the noise effects of very frequent words. A variety of methods are commonly available in the literature [C. J. van Rijsbergen, 1975] for stop-word removal. Typically, commonly available stop word lists about 300 to 400 words are used for the retrieval process.

In addition, words which occur extremely infrequently can also be removed from the collection. This is because such words do not add anything to the similarity computations which are used in most clustering methods. In some cases, such words may be misspellings or typographical errors in documents.

Noisy text collections which are derived from the web, blogs or social networks are more likely to contain such terms. Some lines of research define document frequency based selection purely on the basis of very infrequent terms, because these terms contribute the least to the similarity calculations. However, it should be emphasized that very frequent words should also be removed, especially if they are not discriminative between clusters.

In the TF-IDF scheme [Salton and McGill, 1983], a basic vocabulary of "words" or "terms" is chosen for each document in the corpus, a count is formed of the number of occurrences of each word. Note that the Term Frequency Inverse Document Frequency weighting method can also naturally filter out very common words in a "soft" way. Clearly, the standard set of stop words provide a valid set of words to prune. Nevertheless, quantifying the importance of a term directly to the clustering process, this is essential for more aggressive pruning. A number of such methods are discussing below.

Term Strength: A much more aggressive technique for stop-word removal has been proposed [A. McCallum and K. Nigam, 1998]. The core idea of this approach is to extend techniques which are used in supervised learning to the unsupervised case. The term strength is essentially used to measure how informative a word is for identifying two related documents.

For example, for two related documents x and y, the term strength $s(t)$ of term t is defined in terms of the following probability:

$$s(t) = P(t \in y | t \in x).$$

Clearly, the main issue is how one might define the document x and y as related. One possibility is to use manual (or user) feedback to define when pair of documents is related. This is essentially equivalent to utilizing supervision in the feature selection process and may be practical in situations in which pre-defined categories of documents are available. On the other hand, it is not practical to manually create related pairs in large collections in a comprehensive way. It is therefore desirable to use an automated and purely unsupervised way to define the concept of when a pair of documents is related. It is possible to use automated similarity functions such as the cosine function [G. Salton, 1983; J. Wilbur and K. Sirotkin, 1992] to define the relatedness of document pairs.

Pair of documents is defined to be related if their cosine similarity is above a user-defined threshold. In such cases, the term strength $s(t)$ can be defined by randomly sampling of a number of pairs of such related documents as follows:

$$s(t) = \frac{\text{Number of pairs in which } t \text{ occurs in both}}{\text{Number of pairs in which } t \text{ occurs in the first of the pair}}$$

The first document of the pair may simply be picked randomly. In order to prune features, the term strength may be compared to the expected strength of a term which is randomly distributed in the training documents with the same frequency. If the term strength of t is not at least two standard deviations greater than that of the random word, then it is removed from the collection.

Term Contribution: The concept of term contribution [T. Liu et al., 2003] is based on the fact that the results of text clustering are highly dependent on document similarity. Therefore, the contribution of a term can be viewed as its contribution to document similarity. For example, in the case of dot-product based similarity, the similarity between two documents is defined as the dot product of their normalized frequencies. Therefore, the contribution of a term of the similarity of two documents is the product of their normalized frequencies in the two documents. This needs to be summed over all pairs of documents in order to determine the term contribution. This method requires $O(n2)$ time for each term and therefore sampling methods may be required to speed up the contribution. A major criticism of this method is that it tends to favour highly frequent words without regard to the specific discriminative power within a clustering process.

In most of these methods, the optimization of term selection is based on some pre-assumed similarity functions (e.g., cosine). While this strategy makes these methods unsupervised, there is a concern that the term selection might be biased due to the potential bias of the assumed similarity function. That is, if a different similarity function is assumed, may end up having different results for term selection. Thus, the choice of an appropriate similarity function may be important for these methods.

2.5. Clustering Algorithms

Clustering is a task for which many algorithms have been proposed. No clustering technique is universally applicable, and different techniques are in favor for different clustering purposes. So an understanding of both the clustering problem and the clustering technique is required to apply a suitable method to a given problem.

In the following general parameters of a clustering technique which are relevant to the task of inducing a verb classification.

Parametric Design

Assumptions may (but need not) be made about the form of the distribution used to model the data by the cluster analysis. The parametric design should be chosen with respect to the nature of the data. It is often convenient to assume, for example, that the data can be modeled by a multivariate Gaussian.

Position, Size, Shape and Density of the Clusters

The experimenter might have an idea about the desired clustering results with respect to the position, size, shape and density of the clusters. Different clustering algorithms have different impact on these parameters, as the description of the algorithms will show. Therefore, varying the clustering algorithm influences the design parameters.

Number of Clusters

The number of clusters can be fixed if the desired number is known beforehand (e.g. because of a reference to a gold standard), or can be varied to find the optimal cluster analysis. As Duda et al., [2000] state, 'In theory, the clustering problem can be solved by exhaustive enumeration, since the sample set is finite, so there are only a finite number of possible partitions; in practice, such an approach is unthinkable for all but the simplest problems, since there are at the order of $K^n/K!$ ways of partitioning a set of n elements into k subsets'.

Ambiguity

Verbs can have multiple senses, requiring them being assigned to multiple classes. This is only possible by using a soft clustering algorithm, which defines cluster membership probabilities for the clustering objects. A hard clustering algorithm performs a yes/no decision on object membership and cannot model verb ambiguity, but it is easier to use and interpret.

Many different clustering algorithms have been proposed and tried for document clustering. Clustering algorithms may be divided into groups on several grounds [Jain et al., 1999]. Hierarchical algorithms produce a hierarchy of clusters, while partitioning algorithms give a flat partition of the set. In a hard clustering, each object belongs to only one cluster. When objects belong to more than one cluster (usually with a degree of membership) one talks about a fuzzy clustering.

2.5.1. *Partitioning Algorithms*

Partitioning methods relocate instances by moving them from one cluster to another, starting from an initial partitioning. Such methods typically require that the number of clusters will be pre-set by the user. To achieve global optimality in partitioned-based clustering, an exhaustive enumeration process of all possible partitions is required. Because this is not feasible, certain greedy heuristics are used in the form of iterative optimization. Namely, a relocation method iteratively relocates points between the k clusters.

Given a database of n objects and K, the number of clusters to form, a partitioning algorithm organizes the objects into K partitions ($K \leq n$), where each partition represents a cluster. The clusters are formed to optimize an objective partitioning criterion, often called a similarity function, such as distance, so that objects within a cluster are similar whereas objects of different clusters are dissimilar in terms of the database attributes.

The most well-known and commonly used partitioning methods are K-means method [J. MacQueen, 1967] where each cluster is represented by the mean value of the objects in the cluster, K-medoids method [L.Kaufman and P.J.Rousseeuw, 1990] where each cluster is represented by one of the objects located near the center of the cluster and K-modes method [Z.Huang, 1998] to handle categorical data.

Error Minimization Algorithms

These algorithms, which tend to work well with isolated and compact clusters, are the most intuitive and frequently used methods. The basic idea is to find a clustering structure that minimizes a certain error criterion which measures the "distance" of each instance to its representative value. The most well-known criterion is the Sum of Squared Error (SSE), which measures the total squared Euclidian distance of instances to their representative values. SSE may be globally optimized by exhaustively enumerating all partitions, which is very time-consuming, or by giving an approximate solution (not necessarily leading to a global minimum) using heuristics. The latter option is the most common alternative. The simplest and most commonly used algorithm, employing a squared error criterion is the K means algorithm. This algorithm partitions the data into K clusters (C_1, C_2... C_k) represented by their centers or means. The center of each cluster is calculated as the mean of all the instances belonging to that cluster.

Figure 2.4 presents the pseudo-code of the K means algorithm. The algorithm starts with an initial set of cluster centers, chosen at random or according to some heuristic procedure. In each iteration, each instance is assigned to its nearest cluster center according to the Euclidean distance between the two. Then the cluster centers are re-calculated. A number of convergence conditions are possible. For example, the search may stop when the partitioning error is not reduced by the relocation of the centers. This indicates that the present partition is locally optimal. Other stopping criteria can be used also such as exceeding a pre-defined number of iterations.

Input: S (instance set), K (number of cluster)

Output: clusters

1: Initialize K cluster centers

2: **while** termination condition is not satisfied **do**

3:     Assign instances to the closest cluster center

4:     Update cluster centers based on the assignment

5: **end while**

Figure 2.4: K-means Algorithm

The K -means algorithm may be viewed as a gradient-decent procedure, which begins with an initial set of K cluster-centers and iteratively updates it so as to decrease the error function. A rigorous proof of the finite convergence of the K means type an algorithm is given in [Selim and Ismail, 1984]. The complexity of T iterations of the K -means algorithm performed on a sample size of m instances, each characterized by N attributes is, O (T* K * m* N).

This linear complexity is one of the reasons for the popularity of the K means algorithms. Even if the number of instances is substantially large (which often is the case nowadays), this algorithm is computationally attractive. Thus, the K means algorithm has an advantage in comparison to other clustering methods (e.g. hierarchical clustering methods), which have non-linear complexity. Other reasons for the algorithm's popularity are its ease of interpretation, simplicity of implementation, speed of convergence and adaptability to sparse data [Dhillon and Modha, 2001]. The Achilles heel of the K-means algorithm involves the selection of the initial partition. The algorithm is very sensitive to this selection, which may make the difference between global and local minimum.

Being a typical partitioning algorithm, the K-means algorithm works well only on data sets having isotropic clusters, and is not as versatile as single link algorithms, for instance. In addition, this algorithm is sensitive to noisy data and outliers (a single outlier can increase the squared error dramatically); it is applicable only when mean is defined (namely, for numeric attributes); and it requires the number of clusters in advance, which is not trivial when no prior knowledge is available.

The use of the K-means algorithm is often limited to numeric attributes. Haung [1998] presented the K prototypes algorithm, which is based on the K-means algorithm but removes numeric data limitations while preserving its efficiency. The algorithm clusters objects with numeric and categorical attributes in a way similar to the K means algorithm. The similarity measure on numeric attributes is the square Euclidean distance; the similarity measure on the categorical attributes is the number of mismatches between objects and the cluster prototypes.

Another partitioning algorithm, which attempts to minimize the SSE is the K medoids or PAM (partition around medoids - [Kaufmann and Rousseeuw, 1987]). This algorithm is very similar to the K means algorithm. It differs from the latter mainly in its representation of the different clusters. Each cluster is represented by the most centric object in the cluster, rather than by the implicit mean that may not belong to the cluster.

The K medoids method is more robust than the K means algorithm in the presence of noise and outliers because a medoid is less influenced by outliers or other extreme values than a mean. However, its processing is more costly than the K means method. Both methods require the user to specify K, the number of clusters. Other error criteria can be used instead of the SSE. Estivill-Castro [2000] analyzed the total absolute error criterion. Namely, instead of summing up the squared error, he suggests to summing up the absolute error. While this criterion is superior in regard to robustness, it requires more computational effort.

Given a database of n objects and K, the number of clusters to form, a partitioning algorithm organizes the objects into K partitions ($K \leq n$), where each partition represents a cluster. The clusters are formed to optimize an objective partitioning criterion, often called a similarity function, such as distance, so that objects within a cluster are similar whereas objects of different clusters are dissimilar in terms of the database attributes.

The perhaps most common clustering algorithm is K-Means which is described in most texts on clustering [Jain et al., 1999]. Figure 2.5 gives the basic algorithm and each step may be elaborated with different outcomes and there exists many variants. The most well-known and commonly used partitioning methods are K-means method [J. MacQueen, 1967] where each cluster is represented by the mean value of the objects in the cluster, K-medoids method [L.Kaufman and P.J.Rousseeuw, 1990] where each cluster is represented by one of the objects located near the center of the cluster and K-modes method [Z.Huang, 1998] to handle categorical data.

---

1. Pick k objects at random and let them define k clusters.
2. Calculate cluster representatives.
3. Make new clusters, one per cluster representative. Let each text belongs to the cluster with the most similar cluster representative.
4. Repeat from 2 until a stopping criterion is reached.

Figure 2.5: K-Means Algorithm

The first step defines a random initial partition. There are many other ways of constructing it and the result depends on which one is used. As cluster representative, the mean (the centroid) of the objects in the cluster is usually used. When the clustering is fuzzy, objects may belong to several clusters and thus the cluster representative may be calculated taking this into consideration. The stopping criterion is normally when no objects change clusters or when very few change clusters between iterations. It may also be to stop after a pre-defined number of iterations, since most quality improvement, usually, is gained during the first iterations.

The time complexity of the K-Means algorithm is $O\ (knI)$, where k is the number of clusters, n the number of objects and I the number of iterations (which is dependent on the stopping criterion). In each iteration, the cluster representatives and the kn similarities between all objects and all clusters must be computed [Hand et al., 2001]. The K-Means algorithm requires a number of clusters as input. That is, one has to guess the appropriate number. Of course, it is possible to run the algorithm with several different numbers of clusters and report only the clustering with the best result (as measured by, for instance, the criterion function).

In a general partitioning algorithm, both splitting and division of clusters are allowed and theoretically the result has the optimal number of clusters. Partitioning clustering may be viewed as an optimization problem. An instance is a particular clustering setting: a set of objects, a representation with a similarity measure and a number of clusters and an assignment is a clustering in this view. The objective or criterion, function returns a value for all clustering and the goal is to find a clustering with an optimal value. In most cases, to find such a clustering would require an exhaustive search and most partitioning clustering algorithms are local search strategies that are only guaranteed to find a local optimum.

2.5.2. Hierarchical Algorithms

A hierarchical clustering method works by grouping data into a tree of clusters. Hierarchical clustering methods can be further classified into agglomerative and divisive hierarchical clustering, depending on whether the hierarchical decomposition is formed in a bottom-up or top-down fashion.

Agglomerative Hierarchical Clustering

This bottom-up strategy starts by placing each object in its own cluster and then merges these atomic clusters into larger and larger clusters, until all of the objects are in a single cluster or until certain termination conditions are satisfied.

Divisive Hierarchical Clustering

This top-down strategy does the reverse of agglomerative hierarchical clustering by starting with all objects in one cluster. It subdivides the cluster into smaller and smaller pieces, until each object forms a cluster on its own or until it satisfied certain termination conditions such as a desired number of clusters is obtained or the distance between the two closest clusters is above a certain threshold distance. The methods introduced in this category are: density-based and Grid-based [T. Zhang et al., 1996; S. Guha et al., 1998]

Density-based Methods

The general idea is to continue growing the given cluster as long as the density (number of objects or data) in the neighborhood exceeds some threshold; that is, for each data point within a given cluster, the neighborhood of a given radius has to contain at least a minimum number of points [M. Ester et al., 1998; M. Ankerst et al., 1999].

Grid-based Methods

Grid-based methods divide the object space into a finite number of cells that form a grid structure on which all of the operations for clustering are performed [W. Wang et al., 1997; G. Sheikholeslami et al., 1998; R. Agrawal et al., 1998]. Grid-based clustering methods quantize the space into a finite number of cells that form a grid structure and then all of the clustering operations are performed on this grid structure. The computational complexity of all of the previously mentioned clustering methods is at least linearly proportional to the number of objects. The unique property of grid-based clustering approach is that its computational complexity is independent of the number of data objects but dependent only on the number of cells in each dimension in the quantized space.

STatistical Information Grid (STING) [Wang et al., 1997] is a typical grid-based clustering method which divides the spatial area into rectangular cells. The algorithm constructs several levels of such rectangular cells and these cells form a hierarchical structure; i.e. each cell is partitioned to form a number of cells at the next lower level and Figure 2.6 illustrates the idea.

Statistical information such as means, maximum and minimum values of each grid cell are pre-computed and stored for later query processing. The clustering quality of STING highly depends on the granularity of the lowest level of the grid structure. If the granularity is too coarse then the accuracy of clustering solution will degrade. However, if the granularity is too fine, the processing time will increase drastically. Another limitation of STING is that it can only represent clusters in either horizontal or vertical rectangular shape. Although this method is efficient, its limitations substantially lower than the accuracy of the clustering result.

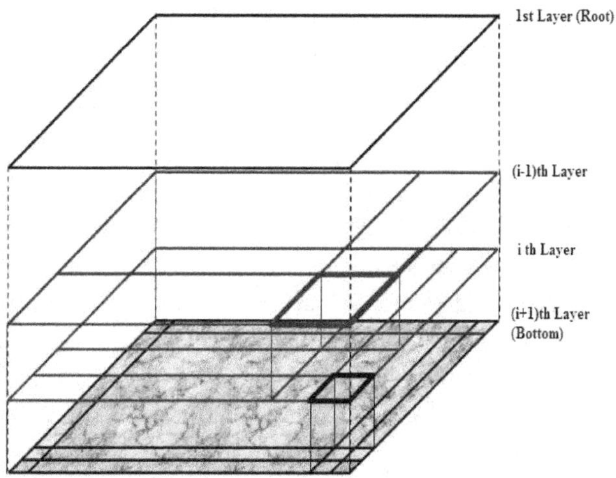

Figure 2.6: Hierarchical Structures for STING Clustering

Constraint-based Method

In this method, the clustering is performed by the incorporation of user or application-oriented constraints. A constraint refers to the user expectation or the properties of desired clustering results. Constraints provide us with an interactive way of communication with the clustering process. Constraints can be specified by the user or the application requirement.

Centroid-based

In this type of grouping method, every cluster is referenced by a vector of values. Each object is part of the cluster whose value difference is minimal, comparing to other clusters. The number of clusters should be pre-defined, and this is the biggest problem of this kind of algorithms. This methodology is the most close to the classification subject and is vastly used for optimization problems.

Distributed-based

Related to pre-defined statistical models, the distributed methodology combines objects whose values belong to the same distribution. Because of its random nature of value generation, this process needs a well defined and complex model to interact in a better way with real data. However these processes can achieved a optimal solution and calculate correlations and dependencies.

Connectivity-based

On this type of algorithm, every object is related to its neighbors, depending the degree of that relationship on the distance between them. Based on this assumption, clusters are created with nearby objects, and can be described as a maximum distance limit. With this relationship between members, these clusters have hierarchical representations. The distance function varies on the focus of the analysis.

Statistical information such as means, maximum and minimum values of each grid cell are pre-computed and stored for later query processing. The clustering quality of STING highly depends on the granularity of the lowest level of the grid structure. If the granularity is too coarse then the accuracy of clustering solution will degrade. However, if the granularity is too fine, the processing time will increase drastically. Another limitation of STING is that it can only represent clusters in either horizontal or vertical rectangular shape. Although this method is efficient, its limitations substantially lower than the accuracy of the clustering result.

Hierarchical algorithms build a cluster hierarchy; clusters are composed of clusters. This may be either all the way from single documents up to the whole text set or any part of this complete structure. There are two natural ways of constructing such a hierarchy: bottom-up and top-down. The first principle is used in agglomerative algorithms and the second in divisive algorithms. The stopping criterion for both algorithms may be that the desired number of cluster is reached or some limit on a criterion function or any internal evaluation measure.

The result of agglomerative clustering is strongly dependent on the similarity measure. The single-link method defines the similarity between two clusters as the similarity between the two most similar objects, one from each cluster. This may result in elongated, locally similar clusters. For equally sized clusters (in volume), the complete-link method is a better choice.

The similarity between two clusters is defined as the similarity between the two most dissimilar objects, one from each cluster. Between these opposites, there are several other measures: the centroid measure (similarity between cluster centroids) [Sips M. et al., 2009], the group average measure and Ward's measure [Hand et al., 2001].

The agglomerative algorithms are deterministic, generating the same cluster hierarchy every time. The similarity definition can be viewed as the criterion function, although, it is used locally for each merging and not as a global score.

The time complexity of the agglomerative algorithms are O(n2) as they all need to compute the similarity between all objects to find the pair of objects that are most similar [Hand et al., 2001]. The steps for computing time complexity of agglomerative clustering are shown in Figure 2.7.

1.   Construct one cluster for each document.

2.   Join the t most similar clusters.

3.   Repeat step 2 until a stopping criterion is reached.

Figure 2.7: Agglomerative Clustering, Usually t = 2

In the divisive algorithms any partitioning algorithm can be applied to split clusters (step 2). The Bisecting K-Means algorithm [Steinbach et al., 2000] is a divisive algorithm for document clustering that uses the K-Means algorithm to split the worst cluster into two.

The time complexity for the Bisecting K-Means algorithm (O (log (k) nl)) is lower than for the K-means algorithm as it does not compare all objects to all cluster representatives. The steps for computing time complexity of divisive clustering are shown in Figure 2.8.

1. Put all documents into one cluster.

2. Split one cluster (the worst) in t new.

3. Repeat step 2 until a stopping criterion is reached.

Figure 2.8: Divisive Clustering, Usually t = 2

Advantages of hierarchical clustering include:

- Flexibility regarding the level of granularity
- Ease of handling any form of similarity or distance
- Applicability to any attribute types

Disadvantages of hierarchical clustering are related to:

- Vagueness of termination criteria
- Most hierarchical algorithms do not revisit (intermediate) clusters once constructed

2.6. Categorical Data Clustering

In this research work, a detailed study has been made on the clustering techniques of Data Mining with attention to Categorical Data Clustering. Then, the techniques such as ROCK, STIRR, Modified STIRR and K-modes are analyzed for implementing the categorical data clustering and the drawbacks of the traditional methods.

STIRR generalizes the powerful methodology of spectral graph partitioning [Gibson et al., 1998] to produce a clustering technique applicable to arbitrary collections of sets. Spectral graph partitioning gives good separators of graph to which they are applied [Spielman 1998]. Spectral graph partitioning uses eigenvectors of adjacency matrices of graphs to find partitions. The vertices are split according to their corresponding value in the Eigen vector and it generalizes this method for relational data in the database which is more complex than a graph thus avoiding combinatorial explosion encountered in existing techniques. STIRR algorithm approaches the problem of clustering as viewing each tuple in the database as a set of items. It uses pure co-occurrence information among items to guide the clustering without imposing any additional priori structure. STIRR uses a weight propagation scheme which is viewed as a type of non-linear dynamical system derived from the table of categorical data. This dynamical system converges very fast typically linear in size of the data. If the convergence cannot be guaranteed, then the clustering task may not be able to stop at a solution.

Modified STIRR developed by Zhang [2000] defines a new configuration updating algorithm for clustering categorical dataset which guarantees convergence and a new normalization scheme has been proposed. Normalization is associated with all attribute values so that squares of all attribute values for an attribute sum up to one. Unlike Gibson [1998], normalization is performed on each field so that the square of their attribute values sum up to one and this would favor fields with fewer attribute values. The Modified STIRR algorithm is an improvement in the above mentioned STIRR algorithm and it overcomes both drawbacks of the STIRR method and is considered to be an overall improvement to the STIRR algorithm. Basically, this algorithm changes a few steps in the above explained STIRR algorithm to achieve its purpose.

The two most important changes it incorporates are:

1. The weight updates are slightly different.
2. The normalization occurs on distinct values (nodes) of the dataset which is taken as a whole. That is, all attributes are normalized together. No separate normalization occurs for each attribute.

ROCK is a robust clustering algorithm for categorical attributes [Guha, 1999]. Since, the distance measures for similarity between points are not appropriate for categorical attributes; this algorithm proposes a novel concept of links to measure the similarity or proximity between two data points. It employs links and not distances when merging clusters. It generates better quality clusters than traditional algorithms but also exhibits good scalability properties. The notion of links between data points helps to overcome the problems with distances. Pair of points are said to be neighbors if their similarity exceeds a certain threshold. The number of links between a pair of points is then, the number of common neighbors for the points. Points belonging to a cluster have a large number of neighbors and thus large number of links [Guha, 1999]. Unlike the distances and similarity between a pair of points which are local properties involving only the two points in question, the link concept incorporates global information about the other points in the neighborhood of the two points. Unlike that of STIRR [Gibson 1998], this algorithm clusters the transactions whereas STIRR clusters the item sets and not transactions in the database.

ROCK is hierarchical clustering algorithms which create a hierarchical decomposition of the objects and they are either **agglomerative** (*bottom-up*) or **divisive** (*top-down*). *Agglomerative* algorithms start with each object, being a separate cluster itself and successively merge groups according to a distance measure. The clustering may stop when all objects are in a single group or at any other point the user wants. These methods generally follow a greedy-like bottom-up merging. ROCK not only generates better quality clusters than traditional algorithms but also exhibits good scalability properties. *Divisive* algorithm is a top-down strategy which starts with all objects in one cluster and clusters are subdivided into smaller and smaller clusters until each object forms a cluster on its own and also certain termination conditions are satisfied.

K-Modes algorithm is an extension of K-Means clustering algorithm, but the working principle of both is same. Instead of means, modes are used in k-modes. By varying the dissimilarity measure, fuzzy K-Modes, K-representative and K-histogram are developed. In fuzzy K-Modes, instead of hard centroid, soft centroid is used [Dae-won kim, et al., 2004]. In K-representative algorithm, the measure relative frequency is used. Ohn Mar San Frequency of attribute value in the cluster divided by cluster length is used as a measure in K-representative [Dae-won kim et al., 2004]. K-Modes is extended with fuzzy, genetic and fuzzy-genetic concepts. A new weighted dissimilarity measure for K-Modes was proposed based on the ratio of frequency of attribute values in the cluster and in the data set. The new weighted measure is experimented with the data sets obtained from the UCI data repository. The results are compared with K-Modes and K-representative which show that the new measure generates clusters with high purity S.Aranganayagi and K.Thangavel [2009].

2.7. Comparison of ROCK, STIRR, Modified STIRR and K-Mode Algorithms

The STIRR algorithm, as implemented by Ganti et al.,[1998] was also benchmarked. STIRR outputs the non-principal basins, i.e. weighted vertices that identify the cluster projection on each attribute. The ROCK algorithm does not lend itself and the ROCK data format assumes that the similarities between data points are given. The practical application of ROCK is thus limited to datasets of well below 10000 records. Following is the complexity and execution time of the algorithms proposed by Mathew Felix [2003] and the approximate complexity and execution time for the benchmark data set.

Table 2.4: Comparison Table for STIRR, Modified STIRR, ROCK and K-Modes

ALGORITHMS	EXECUTION TIME	COMPLEXITY
STIRR	250223 ms	$O(n)$
MODIFIED STIRR	240221 ms	$O(n)$
ROCK	200786 ms	$O(n^2+nm_m m_a+n^2 \log n)$
K-Modes	180456 ms	$O(tkn)$

where n – Number of input data points

k – Number of clusters

t – Number of iteration

m_m – Maximum number of neighbours

m_a – Average number of neighbours.

From the above Figure 2.9 and Table 2.4, it is observed that STIRR generated best clusters and it is suited for most dataset and the ROCK needs more attributes to be more effective. The k-mode algorithm which is an extension of k-means algorithm performs better as compared to hierarchical algorithm and takes less time for execution.

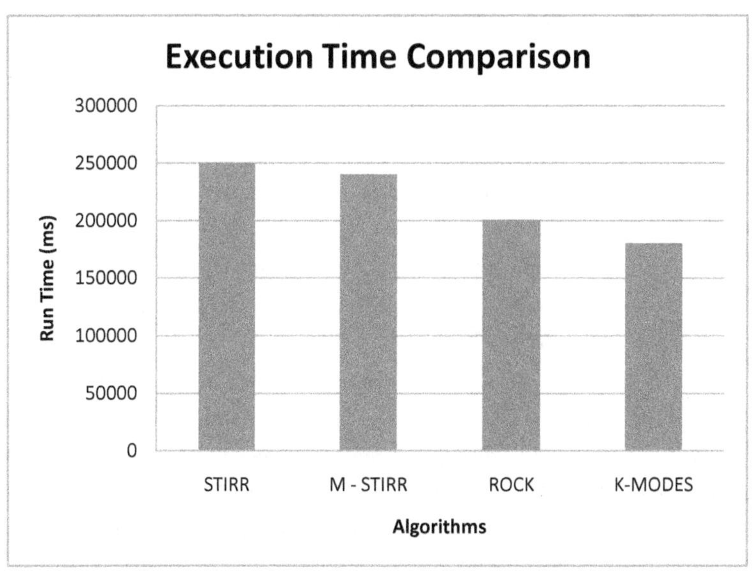

Figure 2.9: Execution Time Comparison Chart

2.7.1. *Comparison of k-means and Hierarchical Algorithms*

The k-means algorithm is well known for its efficiency in clustering large data sets. However, working only on numeric values prohibits it from being used to cluster real world data containing categorical values. Two algorithms which extend the k-means algorithm to categorical domains and domains with mixed numeric and categorical values. The k-modes algorithm uses a simple matching dissimilarity measure to deal with categorical objects replaces the means of clusters with modes and uses a frequency based method to update modes in the clustering process to minimise the clustering cost function. With these extensions, the k-modes algorithm enables the clustering of categorical data in a fashion similar to k-means. The k-prototypes algorithm, through the definition of a combined dissimilarity measure, further integrates the k-means and k-modes algorithms to allow for clustering objects described by mixed numeric and categorical attributes. The two algorithms are efficient when clustering large data set which is *critical* to data mining applications.

Manpreet kaur and Usvir Kaur [2013] proved that k-mean algorithm performs better as compared to hierarchical algorithm and takes less time for execution. But on the other hand, hierarchical algorithm provides good quality of results corresponding to k-mean.

After analyzing both the algorithms with query redirection technique, the authors concluded the following results:

- As the number of records increase the performance of hierarchical algorithm goes decreasing and time for execution is increased.
- K-mean algorithm also increases its time of execution but as compared to hierarchical algorithm its performance is better.
- Hierarchical algorithm shows more quality as compared to k-mean algorithm.
- As a general conclusion, k-mean algorithm is good for large dataset and hierarchical is good for small datasets.

The k-means algorithm is the most extensively studied clustering algorithm and is generally effective in producing good results. The major drawback of this algorithm is that it produces different clusters for different sets of values of the initial centroids. Quality of the final clusters heavily depends on the selection of the initial centroids. The k-means algorithm is computationally expensive and requires time proportional to the product of the number of data items, number of clusters and the number of iterations. Several attempts have been made by researchers to improve the effectiveness and efficiency of the k-means algorithm [Huang Z, 1998; Yuan F et al., 2004 ; Fahim A.M, Salem A. M, Torkey A and Ramadan M. A 2006].

The k-means algorithm has the following important properties:

1. It is efficient in processing large data sets.
2. It often terminates at a local optimum [MacQueen, 1967; Selim and Ismail, 1984].
3. It works only on numeric values.
4. The clusters have convex shapes [Anderberg, 1973].

There exist a few variants of the k-means algorithm which differs in selection of the initial k-means, dissimilarity calculations and strategies to calculate cluster means [Anderberg, 1973; Bobrowski and Bezdek, 1991].

The sophisticated variants of the k-means algorithm include the well-known ISODATA algorithm [Ball and Hall, 1967] and the fuzzy k-means algorithms [Ruspini, 1969, 1973; Bezdek, 1981]. One difficulty in using the k-means algorithm is that the number of clusters has to be specified [Anderberg, 1973; Milligan and Cooper, 1985]. Some variants like ISODATA include a procedure to search for the best k at the cost of some performance

Like k-means method, the k-modes algorithm also produces locally optimal solutions which are dependent on the selection of the initial modes. The k-prototypes algorithm [Huang Z, 1998] integrates the k-means and k-modes processes for clustering the data. In this method, the dissimilarity measure is defined by taking into account both numeric and categorical attributes. In general, the k-modes algorithm is faster than the k-means and k-prototypes algorithm because it needs less iterations to converge, Zhexue Huang [1998]. The conventional fuzzy k-modes algorithm is capable of efficiently clustering categorical data; however, its use of hard centroids for categorical attributes and a simple distance measure compromise its precision and its ability to correctly classify boundary data [Dae-Won Kim 2004].

2.8.   Model-Based Methods

These methods attempt to optimize the fit between the given data and some mathematical model. Model-based methods follow two major approaches: a statistical approach and neural network approach. In the statistical approach, the attention is focused on statistical multisource analysis by means of a method based on Bayesian classification theory and this method is investigated and extended to take into account the relative reliabilities of the sources of data involved in the classification. This requires a way to characterize and quantify the reliability of a data source which becomes important when looking at the combination of information.

Recently, there has been a great resurgence of research in neural network approach and this approach can be successfully used to classify complex data. Neural network approaches have an advantage over the statistical methods that they are distribution free and no prior knowledge is needed about the statistical distributions of the classes in the data sources in order to apply these methods for classification. The neural network approaches also take care of determining how much weight each data source should have in the classification. A set of weights describes the neural network and these weights are computed in an iterative training procedure. On the other hand, neural network approaches can be very complex computationally need a lot of training samples to be applied successfully and their iterative training procedures usually are slow to converge. Also, neural network approaches have more difficulty than do statistical methods in classifying patterns which are not identical to one or more of the training patterns. The performance of the neural network approaches in classification is therefore more dependent on having representative training samples, whereas the statistical approaches need to have an appropriate model of each class.

The choice of clustering algorithm depends both on the type of data available and on the particular purpose of the application. If cluster analysis is used as a descriptive or exploratory tool, it is possible to try several algorithms on the same data to see what the data may disclose.

2.9. Applications of Cluster Analysis

- Clustering analysis is broadly used in many applications such as market research, pattern recognition, data analysis, and image processing.

- Clustering can also help marketers discover distinct groups in their customer base. And they can characterize their customer groups based on the purchasing patterns.

- In the field of biology, it can be used to derive plant and animal taxonomies, categorize genes with similar functionalities and gain insight into structures inherent to populations.

- Clustering also helps in identification of areas of similar land use in an earth observation database. It also helps in the identification of groups of houses in a city according to house type, value, and geographic location.

- Clustering also helps in classifying documents on the web for information discovery.

- Clustering is also used in outlier detection applications such as detection of credit card fraud.

- As a data mining function, cluster analysis serves as a tool to gain insight into the distribution of data to observe characteristics of each cluster.

Requirements of Clustering in Data Mining

The following points throw light on why clustering is required in data mining –

- **Scalability** – Need highly scalable clustering algorithms to deal with large databases.

- **Ability to deal with different kinds of attributes** – Algorithms should be capable to be applied on any kind of data such as interval-based (numerical) data, categorical, and binary data.

- **Discovery of clusters with attribute shape** – the clustering algorithm should be capable of detecting clusters of arbitrary shape. They should not be bounded to only distance measures that tend to find spherical cluster of small sizes.

- **High dimensionality** – the clustering algorithm should not only be able to handle low-dimensional data but also the high dimensional space.

- **Ability to deal with noisy data** – Databases contain noisy, missing or erroneous data. Some algorithms are sensitive to such data and may lead to poor quality clusters.

- **Interpretability** – the clustering results should be interpretable, comprehensible, and usable.

Summary

The functionalities and steps involved in the k-means, k-modes, STIRR and ROCK algorithms are discussed. Due to the limitations of the k-means algorithm, k-modes algorithm has been developed because k-means algorithm does not support categorical data. It measures the dissimilarities between the two nodes and also minimizes the cost functions [Topchy et al, 2003]. The ROCK is a robust hierarchical clustering algorithm which employs links and not distances when merging clusters. This method extends non-metric similarity measures and cluster with the categorical attributes which produce quality cluster rather than the traditional approaches [Anil K.Jain and Richard C.Dubes 1988]. STIRR is an effective algorithm that clusters the attribute values and it is efficient in processing intra-attribute value clustering [Gibson et al., 1998].

The solution produced by the existing algorithms like STIRR, ROCK and k-modes are not effective on above mentioned problems. In the high dimensional vector space, every aspect corresponds to a unique keyword. Along with this, the problem of extracting representative sentences from text is also not effective. Towards this end, it is necessary to develop a novel fuzzy based clustering algorithm for categorical clustering.

The fuzzy based categorical text clustering algorithm for checking famous quotes and to produce effective text clustering where the same meaning can be phrased in various ways. While matching the similarity, the shorter sentences are less effective. Generally, the text clustering mainly focuses on reducing dimensionality, removing irrelevant data, increasing learning accuracy and improving result comprehensibility. Because the time consuming process from entire database can be reduced by making that into clusters which is based on the relationship between the sentences.

Review Questions

1. What is knowledge discovery?. Explain its process.
2. Discuss about the data ware house architecture in detail.
3. Briefly explain the information retrieval methodologies and its type.
4. What is association mining? Explain.
5. Explain the functionality of association mining.

CHAPTER 3

TEXT CLUSTERING METHODS

3.1. Introduction

Data mining is the process of extracting patterns as well as predicting trends from large quantities of data by posing automatically repeated queries [Chris Clifton and Bhavani Thuraisingham, 2001]. During the past decade, data mining has emerged as a technology area for a wide range of applications. The text clustering is the process of grouping information based on the query given by the user and information retrieval in large database which undergoes several processes like pre-processing, extracting and filtering. A real-time example is that a search engine's response to a user query after analyzing thousands of web pages and the major drawback in this process is identifying the accurate page. To overcome this problem, clustering approach enables automatic grouping of related pages based on the user search. But the process of grouping relevant pages is difficult without changing the meaning. Moreover, the duplication of entries in the memory increases the storage complexity as well as time complexity while searching an answer for a query. Hence, this research aims to provide a solution for the problem of reducing duplication and minimize the execution time.

On behalf of clustering, it is necessary to provide a solution for the duplication of the entries because the double entered record increases the storage memory and maximizes the execution time. The lengthy execution time of query evaluation leads to delay of services in terms of data mining and this motivated to find an algorithm which identifies the semantically related sentences and to avoid duplication on the given data set. Hence, a novel fuzzy based clustering algorithm has been proposed for famous quotes in order to overcome the duplication problem and to minimize the execution time. The performance analysis of information retrieval by using the proposed algorithm will produce maximum accuracy when compared to the existing techniques. Because the similarities play a vital role in clustering sentences on the prediction in order to produce an efficient result that enables the clustered data more effectual.

3.2. Clustering

Clustering is a Data Mining technique for grouping data points, such that points within a single group/cluster have similar characteristics, while points in different groups are dissimilar. Traditional clustering algorithms that use distances between points for clustering are not appropriate for Boolean and categorical attributes. Clustering algorithms can broadly be classified as partitional or hierarchical [Han and Kamber 2006; Berkhin. P 2006]. Partitional algorithms, partition the document space into a specific number of groups, using the iterative relocation principle. K-means, K-medioids and bisecting k-means [Steinbach, et al., 2000] are few examples of partitional algorithms. Hierarchical clustering algorithms, on the other hand, begin with all the documents in the document space as individual clusters and iteratively merge the most similar clusters. In contrast to this bottom-up approach (also called the agglomerative approach), hierarchical clustering can be top-down (or the divisive approach). It has often been argued that hierarchical clustering yields better quality clusters and partition methods are preferred often because of their linear time complexity. Apart from this, Carpineto et al., [2009] proposed an alternate classification of clustering algorithms based on how well they are prepared to produce sensible, comprehensive and compact cluster labels. However, this classification type is based on clustering as a technique to improve browsing of search results. Nibir Nayan Boraa et al., [2012] implemented versions of the frequent term-based and frequent noun-based clustering algorithms and they found that the heuristics performed at par with or even better than traditional clustering algorithms.

3.2.1. *Frequent Term Based Text Clustering*

Frequent term-based text clustering methods are shown to be a promising approach for high dimensionality clustering in the literature [Beil et al., 2002]. Frequent item sets form the basis of association rule mining. Exploiting the monotonicity property of frequent item sets (each subset of a frequent item set is also frequent) and using data structures supporting the support counting. The set of all frequent item sets are efficiently determined even for large databases. Many different algorithms have been developed for that task including Apriori [Agrawal R. and Srikant R., 1994]. Frequent item sets can also be used for the task of classification. Liu B. et al., [1998] introduced a general method of building an effective classifier from the frequent item sets of a database. Association rules have also been used in creating text summaries. However, the algorithms used are based on the traditional Apriori-like structure that normally performs recursive scans on the entire database to get frequent items and this has been proven to be slow and inefficient. Zaine O. and Antonie M.L., [2002] presented a modification of this approach for the purpose of text classification.

A frequent item-based approach of clustering is promising because it provides a natural way of reducing the large dimensionality of the document vector space. A *term* is any pre-processed word within a document and a document can be considered as a set of terms occurring in that document at least once. The key idea is not to cluster the high-dimensional vector space but to consider only the low-dimensional frequent term sets as cluster candidates.

A well-selected subset of the set of all frequent term sets can be considered as a clustering and a frequent term set is not a cluster (candidate) but only the description of a cluster (candidate). The corresponding cluster itself consists of the set of documents containing all terms of the frequent term set. Unlike in the case of classification, there are no class labels to guide the selection of such a subset from the set of all frequent term sets. Instead, it is proposed to use the mutual overlap of the frequent term sets with respect to their sets of supporting documents (the clusters) to determine a clustering. The reason behind this approach is that a small overlap of the clusters which results in a small classification error, when the clustering is later used for classifying new documents. Frequent term extraction is a preliminary step for the clustering methods. Two well-known methods, Apriori [Agrawal R. and Srikant R., 1994] and FP-growth [Han J. et al., 2000] are discussed below.

3.2.2. *Apriori Method*

The Apriori algorithm [Agrawal R. and Srikant R., 1994] is a well-known method for computing frequent term sets in a database. Corresponding with the concept of transaction data, it treats documents as transactions and words in documents as terms in transactions and it is used to generate frequent itemsets from the database. The Apriori algorithm uses the Apriori principle which says that the item set I containing item set (say) X is never large if item set X is not large [Shruti Aggarwal and Ranveer Kaur, 2013; Jiawei Han and Micheline Kamber, 2001] or all the non-empty subset of frequent item set must be frequent also. The notations used in the algorithm are: k itemset-any itemset which consists of k items, C_k-Set of candidate k itemsets and L_k-Set of large k itemsets (frequent k itemsets). These itemsets are derived for the candidate itemsets in each pass. Based on this principle, the Apriori algorithm generates a set of candidate item sets whose lengths are *(k+1)* from the large k item sets and prune those candidates which does not contain large subset. Then, for the rest of the candidates, only those candidates that satisfy the minimum support threshold (decided previously by the users are taken to be large *(k+1)*-item sets. Apriori algorithms generate item sets by using only the large item sets found in the previous pass, without considering the transactions and the steps involved in the algorithm are:

1. Generate the candidate *1*-itemsets (C_1) and write their support counts during the first scan.
2. Find the large *1*-itemsets (L_1) from C_1 by eliminating all those candidates which does not satisfy the support criteria.

3. Join the L_1 to form C_2 and use Apriori principle and repeat until no frequent itemset is found.

The approach given by Suhani Nagpal [2012] provides a way to improve efficiency and reducing complexity. Firstly, database scanning is performed only once and further temporary tables have been used for scanning purpose. Secondly, it uses logarithmic decoding technique for reducing the complexity Scheme to provide good performance. A method has been proposed to improve the efficiency of Apriori algorithm by using Transaction Reduction [Jaishree Singh et al., 2013]. Typical Apriori algorithm generates a large set of candidate sets if database is large. A new approach has been given for reducing the candidate item sets by reducing the connecting item sets i.e. frequent item sets of previous pass [Jiao Yabing, 2013].

The Apriori algorithm uses a level-wise search where k-term sets are used to explore $(k+1)$ - term sets to mine frequent term sets from the database. Suppose that, there are m frequent 1-term sets and then $\frac{m(m-1)}{2}$ candidate 2-term sets are generated. In addition, the algorithm requires multiple scans of the entire database to check for frequent term sets. More specifically, it requires $(n+1)$ scans, where n is the size of the largest frequent k-term set. These bottlenecks may greatly affect the overall efficiency of frequent term set-based clustering methods. Many variations of the Apriori and frequent term set extraction algorithm have been proposed in the literature to address these weaknesses.

3.2.3. *Frequent Pattern-Growth Method*

To avoid generating a huge set of candidate term sets as in the Apriori algorithm, Han J. et al., [2000] presented an efficient frequent term set extraction algorithm called Frequent-Pattern growth (FP-growth). This algorithm adopts a divide-and-conquer approach to minimize the candidate generation process to only those most likely to be frequent and employs a compact prefix-tree data structure, Frequent-Pattern tree (FP-tree) to avoid repetitive scanning of the database.

The FP-growth algorithm performs exactly two scans of the transaction database and mines on the compact data structure, FP-tree, to find all frequent term sets without generating all possible candidate sets. Han J. et al., [2000] showed that FP-growth is about an order of magnitude faster than Apriori in large databases. Although, the FP-growth algorithm is efficient, sometimes, it is infeasible to construct a main memory-based FP-tree when the database is large which is very common for the case of document clustering.

FP-Growth Algorithm Variations

The popularity and efficiency of FP-Growth Algorithm contributes with many studies that propose variations to improve the performance [Cornelia Gyorödi, et al., 2006; F. Bonchi and B. Goethals, 2004; Aiman Moyaid, et al., 2009; Gao, J., 2007; Grahne, G. and Zhu, J., 2005; Gao, J., 2007; Cornelia Gyorödi, et al., 2003; F. Bonchi, et al., 2003; Balázes Rácz, 2004; Grahne O. and Zhu J, 2004] and some of them are briefly described below.

DynFP-Growth Algorithm

The DynFP-Growth [Cornelia Gyorödi, 2003; Cornelia Gyorödi and Robert Gyorödi, 2006] has focused in improving the FP-Tree algorithm construction based on two observed problems:

1. The resulting FP-tree is not unique for the same "logical" database.
2. The process needs two complete scans of the database.

To solve the first problem Gyorödi C et al., [2003] proposes the usage of a support descending order together with a lexicographic order, ensuring in this way the uniqueness of the resulting FP-tree for different "logically equivalent" databases. To solve the second problem, the authors proposed a dynamic FP-tree reordering algorithm and employing this algorithm whenever a "promotion" to a higher order of at least one item is detected. An important feature in this approach is that it's not necessary to rebuild the FP-Tree when the actual database is updated. It's only needed to execute the algorithm, by taking into consideration the new transactions and the stored FP-Tree. Another adaptation proposed, because of the dynamic reordering process, is a modification in the original structures, by replacing the single linked list with a doubly linked list for linking the tree nodes to the header and adding a master-table to the same header.

FP-Bonsai Algorithm

The FP-Bonsai [F. Bonchi and B. Goethals 2004] improved the FP-Growth performance by reducing (pruning) the FP-Tree using the ExAnte data-reduction technique [F. Bonchi, et al., 2003] and the pruned FP-Tree was called FP-Bonsai.

AFOPT Algorithm

Guimei Liu et al., [2003] investigated the performance of FP-Growth algorithm and proposed the AFOPT algorithm to improve the performance of FP-Growth in the following four perspectives.

- **Item Search Order:** when the search space is divided, all items are sorted in some order. The number of the conditional databases constructed can differ very much by using different items search orders.

- **Conditional Database Representation:** the traversal and construction cost of a conditional database heavily depends on its representation.

- **Conditional Database Construction Strategy:** constructing every conditional database physically can be expensive, affecting the mining cost of each individual conditional database.

- **Tree Traversal Strategy:** the traversal cost of a tree is minimal by using top-down traversal strategy.

NONORDFP Algorithm

The Nonordfp algorithm [Balázes Rácz, 2004; Cornelia Gyorödi et al., 2006] motivated by the running time and the space required for the FP-Growth algorithm. The theoretical difference is the main data structure (FP-Tree) which is more compact and which is not needed to rebuild it for each conditional step. A compact memory efficient representation of an FP-tree by using Trie data structure with memory layout allows faster traversal, faster allocation and optionally, projection was introduced.

FP-Growth Algorithm*

FP-Growth* algorithm was proposed by Grahne O et al., [2004] and Grahne G. et al., [2005] and is based on the conclusion about the usage of CPU time to compute frequent item sets by using FP-Growth and they observed that 80% of CPU time was used for traversing FP-Trees [Aiman Moyaid et al., 2009]. Therefore, they used an array-based data structure combined with the FP-Tree data structure to reduce the traversal time and incorporate several optimization techniques.

PPV, PrePost and FIN Algorithms

Z. H. Deng, et al., [2010], Z. H. Deng, et al., [2012] and Z. H. Deng, et al., [2014] proposed three algorithms namely PPV, PrePost and FIN based on three novel data structures called Node-list [Z. H. Deng, et al., 2010], N-list [Z. H. Deng, et al., 2012] and Nodeset [Z. H. Deng, et al., 2014] respectively for facilitating the mining process of frequent itemsets. The data structures are based on a FP-tree with each node encoding with pre-order traversal and post-order traversal, Compared with Node-lists, N-lists and Nodesets which are more efficient. Traversals cause the efficiency of PrePost and FIN is higher than that of PPV.

3.3. Sentence Level Clustering

The first successful fuzzy relational clustering model is generally considered to be [Hathaway et al., 1989] Relational Fuzzy C-Means (RFCM) algorithm. The family of spectral clustering algorithms [U.V. Luxburg, 2007] which have become very popular over the last decade are based on matrix decomposition techniques. Data points are mapped onto the space defined by the Eigenvectors associated with the top Eigenvalues of the affinity matrix and clustering is then performed in this transformed space, typically by using a k-means algorithm. A fuzzy relational clustering approach is used to produce clusters with sentences where each of them corresponds to some content. The output of clustering indicates the strength of the association among the data elements. Andrew Skabar and Khaled Abdalgader [2013] proposed a novel fuzzy relational clustering algorithm called Fuzzy Relational Eigen Vector Centrality based Clustering Algorithm (FRECCA). To overcome the drawbacks of these clustering algorithms such as instability of clusters, complexity and sensitivity, V. Abinaya et al., [2014] proposed an algorithm called Hierarchical Fuzzy Relational Eigenvector Centrality-based Clustering Algorithm (HFRECCA) as an extension of FRECCA which is used for the clustering of sentences. Contents present in text documents contain hierarchical structure and there are many terms present in the documents which are related to more than one theme. Hence, HFRECCA can be useful algorithm for natural language documents.

Various spectral clustering algorithms have been proposed [J. Shi and J. Malik 2000; M. Meila and J. Shi, 2001; A.Y. Ng, et al., 2001; D. Lee and H. Seung 2001 and S.X. Yu and J. Shi 2003]. Spectral clustering has been applied to sentence clustering   [H. Zha 2002] and Wang et al., [2008] have recently applied a closely related non-negative matrix factorization. Lee. D and Seung. H [2001] introduced a technique to sentence clustering in the context of multi-document summarization. Andrew Skabar [2013] presented a novel fuzzy clustering algorithm that operates on relational input data; i.e. data in the form of a square matrix of pair wise similarities between data objects. The algorithm uses a graph representation of the data and operates in an Expectation-Maximization framework in which the graph centrality of an object in the graph is interpreted as likelihood. Results of applying the algorithm to sentence clustering tasks demonstrate that the algorithm is capable of identifying overlapping clusters of semantically related sentences and that it is therefore of potential use in a variety of text mining tasks.

D. Wang, et al., [2009] proposed multi-document summarization framework which is based on sentence-level semantic analysis and symmetric non-negative matrix factorization. Based on similarity matrix, symmetric non-negative matrix factorization algorithm is used to divide the sentence into groups for extraction. Within cluster sentence, selection is based on both internal (computed similarity between sentences) and external information (given topic information), otherwise performance will not be improved. Kamal Sarkar [2009] proposed multi-document text summarization based on the factors such as clustering the sentences, cluster ordering and selection of representative sentences from clusters. After pre-processing, similarity between sentences is provided by uni-gram matching-based similarity measure. To make system effective and portable in domain and language, pre-processing stemming is not applied on input and features such as length, sentence position and cue phrase are not incorporated.

Y. Li, et al., [2006] presented a method for measuring the similarity between sentences or very short text based on semantic and word order information. Semantic similarity is derived from lexical knowledge base and corpus. Word order similarity measures the number of different words as well as word pairs in different orders. This method is inefficient and requires human input and is not adaptable to all application domains. B.J. Frey and D. Dueck [2007] proposed Affinity Propagation, a technique which simultaneously considers all data points as potential centroids (or exemplars). Frey and Dueck [2007] have showed how Affinity Propagation can be applied to the problem of extracting representative sentences from text.

Fuzzy c-means is a method of clustering which allows one piece of data which belongs to two or more clusters. This method (developed by Dunn [1973] improved by Bezdek [1981]) is frequently used in pattern recognition. It is based on minimization of the following objective function:

$$J_m = \sum_{i=1}^{N} \sum_{j=1}^{C} u_{ij}^{m} \left\| x_i - c_j \right\|^2 \quad \text{where } 1 \leq m \leq \infty$$

where m is any real number greater than 1, u_{ij} is the degree of membership of x_i in the cluster j, x_i is the ith of d-dimensional measured data, c_j is the d-dimension center of the cluster and $||*||$ is any norm expressing the similarity between any measured data and the center.

R.J. Hathaway et al., [1989] proposed Relational Fuzzy c-Means algorithm which is a variant of Fuzzy c-Means and it operates on relational data input. It requires that the relation expressed by this data be Euclidean. R.Mihalcea et al., [2006] proposed Text Rank, a graph-based ranking model for text processing and showed how this model is successfully used in natural language applications. T. Geweniger et al., [2010] proposed Median clustering methodology for prototype based clustering of similarity/dissimilarity data. In Median clustering, the median c-means algorithms with the fuzzy c-means approach are combined which is only applicable for vectorial (metric) data in its original variant.

P. Corsini et al., [2005] proposed an Any Relational Clustering Algorithm (ARCA) based on the popular fuzzy C-means algorithm which does not require any particular restriction on the relation matrix. ARCA partitions the data set by minimizing the Euclidean distance between each object belonging to a cluster and the prototype of the cluster. ARCA determines the optimal partition by minimizing the objective function. A survey on sentence level clustering algorithms has been presented by Sathishkumar K et al., [2013] and the survey explains about the problems in clustering in sentence level and the solutions to overcome those problems. G.Thilagavathi et al., [2014] proposed a fuzzy clustering algorithm that operates on Expectation-Maximization framework in which the cluster membership probabilities for sentence in each cluster are identified. Results obtained while applying the algorithm to sentence clustering tasks demonstrate that the algorithm is capable of identifying overlapping clusters of semantically related sentences.

3.4.   Analysis of Text Clustering Methods

Text clustering (or Document **clustering**) is the application of **cluster** analysis to textual documents. It has applications in automatic document organization, topic extraction and fast information retrieval or filtering. The problem of clustering has been studied widely in the database and statistics literature in the context of a wide variety of data mining tasks [50, 54]. The clustering problem is defined to be that of finding groups of similar objects in the data. The similarity between the objects is measured with the use of a similarity function. The problem of clustering can be very useful in the text domain, where the objects to be clusters can be of different granularities such as documents, paragraphs, sentences or terms. Clustering is especially useful for organizing documents to improve retrieval and support browsing.

Large number of clustering algorithms described in the literature focuses on text clustering and there arises a need for analyzing the algorithms which focuses on categorical text clustering. The following section provides a brief overview about the important categorical text clustering algorithms. The most common cluster algorithms such as K-mode [Zhexue Huang, 1998], RObust Clustering using linKs (ROCK) [Sudipto Guha et al.,1999] and Sieving Through Iterated Relational Reinforcement (STIRR) [David Gibson, Jon M et al.,1998] are discussed below. The difficulties in clustering algorithms are language variability which has same meaning but it is phrased on two ways. By making the sentence smaller it would be exact matching of their terms. By doing this, one can expect the cluster which can be closely matched to the concepts described based on the query terms. But most of the documents have irrelevant details of topics or themes and many sentences will be related to some degree. The calculation between the pair-wise similarities or dissimilarities can be performed with data points that should be done from attribute data based on similarities such as cosine similarity. This can be also applicable for relational clustering algorithms.

3.4.1. *Overview of K-Means and K-Modes Methods*

K-means [MacQueen, 1967] is one of the simplest unsupervised learning algorithms that solve the well known clustering problem. Modification in k-means has been developed by focusing on background knowledge that can be expressed as a set of instance-level constraints on the clustering process.

In the context of text clustering algorithms, instance level constraints are a useful way to express a priori knowledge about which instances should or should not be grouped together. The most common instance level constraints are **Must-link** constraints which specify that two instances have to be in the same cluster and **Cannot-link** constraints which specify that two instances must not be placed in the same cluster. The must-link constraints define a transitive binary relation over the instances. Consequently, when making use of a set of constraints (of both kinds) cannot-link constraints take a transitive closure over the constraints [Kiri Wagsta et al., 2001].

K-means method [L.Kaufman and P.J.Rousseeuw, 1990] has been a very popular technique for partitioning large data sets with numerical attributes. However, data mining applications frequently involve many data sets that also consist of categorical attributes. One approach proposed by H.Ralambondrainy [1995] use the K-means algorithm to cluster categorical data by converting multiple categories attributes into binary attributes (using 0 and 1 to represent either a category absent or present) and treat the binary attributes as numeric. If this algorithm is used in data mining, it needs to handle a large number of binary attributes because categorical attributes in data sets often have hundreds or thousands of categories. This will increase both computational and space costs of the K-means algorithm. Another drawback is that the cluster means, given by real values between 0 and 1 does not really reflect the characteristics of the clusters.

Indeed, in applying K-means method to categorical data, two main problems are encountered, namely, the construction of clusters' centers and the definition of dissimilarity between objects and clusters' centers. The K-modes method [Z.Huang, 1998] is considered as one of the most popular of them and it was proposed to extend the K-means to tackle the problem of clustering large categorical data sets in data mining and this method uses the K-means paradigm to cluster data having categorical values.

K-modes Method Parameters

K-modes method is one of the simplest unsupervised learning algorithms that solve the well-known clustering problem. The K-modes method extends the K-means [L.Kaufman and P.J.Rousseeuw, 1990] one by using a simple matching dissimilarity measure for categorical objects, modes instead of means for clusters and a frequency-based method to update modes in the clustering process to minimize the clustering cost function. The modifications of the K-means algorithm are discussed below.

Given a cluster $\{X_1,...X_p\}$ of p categorical objects with $X_i=(x_{i,1}, .., x_{i,s})$, $1 \le i \le p$, its mode $Q =(q_1, .., q_s)$ is defined by assigning q_j, $1 \le j \le s$, where s is the number of attributes, the category most frequently encountered in $\{x_{1,j}, ..., x_{p,j}\}$. However, the mode of cluster is not generally unique and this makes the algorithm unstable depending on mode selection during the clustering process.

The procedure follows a simple and easy way to classify a given data set through a certain number of clusters (assume K clusters) fixed a priori and the main idea is to define K-modes, one for each cluster. These modes should be placed in a critical way because of different location causes different results. So, the better choice is to place them as much as possible far away from each other. The next step is to take each point belonging to a given data set and associate it to the nearest mode using the simple matching dissimilarity measure. When no point is pending, the first step is completed and an early groupage is done. At this point, it is necessary to recalculate K-new modes of the clusters resulting from the previous step based on frequency-based method. Then, the algorithm has these K-new modes, a new binding has to be done between the same data set points and the nearest new mode and a loop has been generated. As a result of this, loop may notice that the K-modes change their location step by step until no more changes are done and in other words modes do not move any more.

Although it is proved that the procedure will always terminate, the K-modes algorithm does not necessarily find the most optimal configuration, corresponding to the global objective function minimum. The algorithm is also significantly sensitive to the initial randomly selected cluster modes. The K-modes algorithm can be run multiple times to reduce this effect. This algorithm has an input, a pre-defined number of clusters i.e. the K from its name. K-modes algorithm is an iterative procedure in which a crucial concept is the one of mode. Mode is an artificial point in the space of records which represents all objects of the particular cluster. The coordinates of this point are the most frequent occurrences of attribute values that belong to the cluster.

The algorithm is composed of the following steps:

1. Select K initial modes, one for each cluster.

2. Allocate an object to the cluster whose mode is the nearest to it according to the simple matching dissimilarity measure and update the mode of the cluster after each allocation.

3. Once all objects have been allocated to clusters, retest the dissimilarity of objects against the current modes. If an object is found such that its nearest mode belongs to another cluster rather than its current one, reallocate the object to that cluster and update the modes of both clusters.

4. Repeat 3 until no object has changed clusters after a full cycle test of the whole data set.

Consider a classification problem of firm's staff and suppose that a training set T is defined by Table 3.1.

Table 3.1: Training Set T Relative to the Standard K-modes Method

Objects	Qualification	Income	Departments
X_1	A	High	Finance
X_2	B	Low	Finance
X_3	C	Average	Marketing
X_4	C	Average	Accounts
X_5	B	Low	Marketing
X_6	A	High	Finance
X_7	B	Low	Accounts

Suppose that K = 3, 3-partition of T is initialized randomly as follows:

$$C_1 = \{X_1\},\ C_2 = \{X_2\},\ \text{and}\ C_3 = \{X_3\}.$$

The three cluster modes, one for each cluster are defined by:

$Q_1 =$ (A, High, Finance)

$Q_2 =$ (B, Low, Finance)

$Q_3 =$ (C, Average, Marketing)

The k-modes algorithm is simple and understandable and the algorithm converges in a finite number of iterations. This standard version of the K-modes method has some of the weaknesses: ① The ways of initializing the modes was not specified. One popular way to start is to randomly choose the K of the samples. So, the produced results depend on the initial values for the modes. The standard solution is to try a number of different starting points. ② The results depend on the value of K. Unfortunately, there is no general theoretical solution to find the optimal number of clusters for any given data set. A simple approach is to compare the results of multiple runs with different K classes and choose the best one according to a given criterion such that the clustering cost function. 3) The mode of cluster is not generally unique and this makes the algorithm unstable depending on mode selection during the clustering process.

K-modes Method under Uncertainty

Standard versions of the K-modes method and its extensions give good results in a context in which everything is known with certainty. The reality is connected to uncertainty and imprecision by nature and such uncertainty may badly affect the classification performance. However, a good classifier must be able to predict the object's class value even when information concerning the object is imperfect. So, the K-modes are inadequate and badly adapted to ensure its role of classification in an environment characterized by a lot of uncertainty and imprecision. Due to the above stated problems or reasons, researchers are interested in improving or extending this method. The idea of k-modes method with uncertainty is to combine theories managing uncertainty and imprecision with the K-modes method. The theories are probability theory, fuzzy set theory, belief function theory and possibilistic theory. Hence, this adaptation of K-modes method to an uncertain environment has led to a new approach and the fuzzy K-modes method [Z.Huang and M.K.Ng, 1999] was developed. In this approach, one object does not belong exclusively to a well-defined cluster. In fact, it may belong to several clusters with different membership degrees. This extension can be said as fuzzy k-modes method which is briefly presented below.

3.4.2. Fuzzy K-Modes Method

Fuzzy K-modes method deals with cognitive uncertainty and it can take into account imprecision and fuzziness in object class memberships by using fuzzy sets and membership degrees. Fuzzy K-modes approach is a method of clustering which allows one piece of data to belong to two or more clusters. It uses fuzzy partitioning such that a data point can belong to all groups with different membership grades between 0 and 1.

The algorithm is composed of the following steps:

1. Choose an initial point $Q^{(1)}$. Determine a fuzzy partition matrix $W^{(1)}$ such that $P(W, Q^{(1)})$ is minimized and set $t = 1$.

2. Determine $Q^{(t+1)}$ such that $P(W^{(t)}, Q^{(t+1)})$ is minimized.

   If $P(W^{(t)}, Q^{(t+1)}) = P(W^{(t)}, Q(t)) < e$ then STOP; otherwise return to step 3

3. Determine $W^{(t+1)}$ such that $P(W^{(t+1)}, Q^{(t+1)})$ is minimized. If $P(W^{(t+1)}, Q^{(t+1)}) = P(W^{(t)}, Q^{(t+1)}) < e$ then STOP; otherwise set $t = t + 1$ and go to step 2.

The fuzzy K-modes algorithm produces a fuzzy partition matrix W. To obtain the cluster membership from W, the record X_i was assigned to the lth cluster if $w_{i,l}=\max_{1\leq h\leq k}\{w_{i,h}\}$. If the maximum is not unique, then X_i was assigned to the cluster of first achieving the maximum.

3.4.3. ROCK

ROCK is a hierarchical clustering algorithm that explores the concept of links (the number of common neighbors between two objects) for data with categorical attributes. Two distinct clusters may have a few points or outliers that are close; therefore, relying on the similarity between points to make clustering decisions could cause the two clusters to be merged. ROCK takes a more global approach to clustering by considering the neighborhoods of individual pairs of points.If two similar points also have similar neighborhoods, then the two points likely belong to the same cluster and so can be merged [Sudipto Guha et al., 1998].

Figure 3.1: Overview of ROCK

The steps involved in clustering using ROCK are described in Figure 3.1 After drawing a random sample from the database, a hierarchical clustering algorithm that employs links is applied to the sampled points.

Finally, the clusters involving only the sampled points are used to assign the remaining data points on disk to the appropriate clusters. In the following subsections describe the steps performed by ROCK in greater detail.

Overview of the Algorithm

ROCK's hierarchical clustering algorithm is presented in Figure 3.2 and it accepts as input the set S of n sampled points to be clustered (that are drawn randomly from the original data set) and the number of desired clusters k.

```
Procedure cluster(S, k)
begin
1.  link := compute_links(S)
2.  for each s ∈ S do
3.     q[s] := build_local_heap(link, s)
4.  Q := build_global_heap (S,q)
5.  while size(Q) > k do {
6.     u := extract_max(Q)
7.     v := max(q[u])
8.     delete(Q, v)
9.     w := merge(u, v)
10.    for each x ∈ q[u] ∪ q[v] do {
11.       link[x, w] := link[x, u] +link[x, v]
12.       delete(q[x], u); delete(q[x], v)
13.       insert(q[x],w, g(x, w));   insert(q[w], x, g(x, w))
14.       update(Q, x, q[x])
15.    }
16.    insert(Q, w, q[w])
17.    deallocate(q[u]); deallocate(q[v])
18. } End
```

Figure 3.2: Rock Clustering Algorithm

The procedure begins by computing the number of links between pairs of points in Step 1. Initially, each point is a separate cluster. For each cluster i, build a local heap $q[i]$ and maintain the heap during the execution of the algorithm. $q[i]$ contains every cluster j such that assume $[i,j]$ is non-zero. The clusters j in $q[i]$ are ordered in the decreasing order of the goodness measure with respect to i, $g(i,j)$.

The while-loop in Step 5 iterates until only k clusters remain in the global heap Q. In addition, it also stops clustering if the number of links between every pair of the remaining clusters becomes zero. In each step of the while-loop, the max cluster u is extracted from Q by extract_max and $q[u]$ is used to determine the best cluster v for it. Since clusters u and v will be merged, entries for u and v are no longer required and can be deleted from Q. Clusters u and v are then merged in Step 9 to create a cluster w containing $|u|+|v|$ points. There are two tasks that need to be carried out once clusters u and v are merged:

1. For every cluster that contains u or v in its local heap, the elements u and v need to be replaced with the new merged cluster w and the local heap needs to be updated.

2. New local heap for *w* needs to be created. Both these tasks are carried out in the for-loop of Step 10-15. A detailed description of how this for-loop works was given by Sudipto Guha et al., [1998].

```
procedure compute_links(S)

begin

1.  Compute nbrlist[i] for every point i in S

2.  Set link[i, j) to be zero for all i, j

3.  for  i := 1 to  n  do {

4.     N := nbrlist[i]

5.       for j := 1 to  INI - 1 do

6.          for  l:=  j + 1 to  INI do

7.             link[N(j), N(l)) := link[N(j), N(l)) + 1

8.  }

End
```

Figure 3.3: Algorithm for Computing Links

The algorithm in Figure 3.3 provides a more efficient way of computing links. In that, on an average, the number of neighbors for each point will be small compared to the number of input points n, causing the adjacency matrix A to be sparse.

For every point, after computing a list of its neighbors, the algorithm considers all pairs of its neighbors. For each pair, the point contributes one link. If the process is repeated for every point and the link count is incremented for each pair of neighbors, then at the end, the link counts for all pairs of points will be obtained. If m_i is the size of the neighbor list for point i, then for point i and the link count should be increased by one in m_i^2 entries. Thus, the complexity of the algorithm is $\sum_i m_i^2$ which is $O(nm_m m_a)$, where m_a and m_m are the average and maximum number of neighbors for a point, respectively. In the worst case, the value of m_m can be n in which case, the complexity of the algorithm becomes $O(m_a n^2)$. In practice, m_m to be reasonably close to m_a and thus, for these cases, the complexity of the algorithm reduces to $O(m_a^2 n)$ on average.

Time and Space Complexity

Computation of Links: It is possible to compute links among pairs of points in $O(n^{2.37})$ using standard matrix multiplication techniques, or alternatively in $O(n^2 m_a)$ time for average number of neighbors m_a. The space requirement for the link computation is at most $n(n + 1)/2$, when every pair of points are linked. However, in general, not every pair of points will have links between them and expect the storage requirements to be much smaller.

The algorithm can show this to be $O(min\{nm_mm_a, n^2\})$ where m_m is the maximum number of neighbors for a point and this is because a point i can have links to at most min $\{n, m_mm_i\}$ other points. The time to build each local heap initially is $O(n)$ (a heap for a set of n input clusters can be built in time that is linear in the number of clusters [Thomas H et al., 1990]). The global heap also has at most n clusters initially and can be constructed in $O(n)$ time. Next, the complexities of the steps in the while-loop which is executed $O(n)$ times. The inner for-loop dominates the complexity of the while-loop. Since the size of each local queue can be n in the worst case and the new merged cluster w may need to be inserted in $O(n)$ local queues, the time complexity of the for-loop becomes $O(n \log n)$ and that of the while-loop is $O(n^2 \log n)$ in the worst case. Due to the above analysis, ROCK's clustering algorithm, along with computation of neighbor lists and links, has a worst-case time complexity of $O(n^2 + nm_mm_a + n^2 \log n)$.

The space complexity of the algorithm depends on the initial size of the local heaps. The reason for this is that when two clusters are merged, their local heaps are deleted and the size of the new cluster's local heap can be no more than the sum of the sizes of the local heaps of the merged clusters. Since each local heap only contains those clusters to which it has non-zero links, the space complexity of ROCK's clustering algorithm is the same as that of link computation, that is, $O(min\{n^2, nm_mm_a\})$.

Random Sampling

In case the database is large, random sampling enables ROCK to reduce the number of points to be considered and ensures that the input data set fits in main memory. Consequently, significant improvements in execution times for ROCK can be realized. With an appropriate sample size, the quality of the clustering is not sacrificed. On the contrary, random sampling can aid clustering by filtering outliers. Efficient algorithms for selecting random samples from a database are found vastly in the literature [Jeff Vitter,1985]. Also, an analysis of the appropriate sample size for good quality clustering can also be found [Sudipto Guha et al., 1998] and it is noted that the salient feature of ROCK is not sampling but the clustering algorithm that utilizes links instead of distances.

Handling Outliers

In ROCK, outliers can be handled fairly effectively. The first pruning occurs when choose a value for θ and by definition outliers are relatively isolated from the rest of the points. This immediately allows one to discard the points with very few or no neighbors because they will never participate in the clustering and this is the most significant part where outliers are eliminated. However, in some situations, outliers may be present as small groups of points that are loosely connected to the rest of the dataset. This immediately suggests to the researchers that these clusters will persist as small clusters for the most part of clustering. These will only participate in clustering when the number of clusters remaining is actually close to the number of clusters in the data. So, the algorithm should be stopped at a point such that the number of remaining clusters is a small multiple of the expected number of clusters.

In the final labelling phase, ROCK assigns the remaining data points residing on disk to the clusters generated by using the sampled points. This is performed as follows. First, a fraction of points from each cluster i is obtained; Let L_i denote this set of points from cluster i used for labelling. Then, the original data set is read from disk and each point p is assigned to the cluster i such that p has the maximum neighbors in L_i (after normalization). Sudipto Guha et al., [1999] proposed a new concept of links to measure the similarity/proximity between a pair of data points with categorical attributes and this algorithm employs links and not distances for merging clusters.

3.4.4. STIRR Algorithm

A novel approach for clustering collections of sets has been described [Gibson et al, 1998] and its application to the analysis and mining of categorical data. The collection of sets referred as the relational table with each tuple visualized as a set. The STIRR algorithm works on categorical data-fields in tables whose attributes cannot be ordered as numerical values can [Zhang et al, 2000]. As categorical data usually do not have inherent geometric properties, the clustering of categorical data seems more complicated than that of numerical data. Mining of association rules is effective only for items that appear in the same tuple. The STIRR algorithm not only takes into consideration items that appear together in a tuple, but also identifies relationships amongst items occurring in different tuples.

Overview of the Algorithm

- *Iterative method* – The STIRR algorithm is an iterative method and the number of iterations depends upon the dataset in consideration. The algorithm keeps on performing the same steps a number of times until a result is obtained which does not change on further iterations.

- *Assigning and propagating weights on categorical values* - A relational table is taken as input to the algorithm and this relational table has fields (attributes) that can take values in a particular domain. The STIRR algorithm takes each distinct value in the table and performs a series of steps to assign numerical values (weights) to it.

- *Similarity measure obtained from co-occurrence of values in dataset* - Each distinct value in the database is assigned a weight. In the first iteration of the STIRR algorithm, the weight of each distinct value is calculated depending on with what values this distinct value appears in the database. e.g. for the distinct group value "defence", for every tuple in which the group "defence" appears and takes the sum of the target and weapon weights that occur in those tuples and assign this total weight to the "defence" attribute value. This is repeated for all distinct values in the database. Then, in the subsequent iterations, the same procedure is repeated and hence this weight is propagated further – to other targets and weapons and even to other military groups. Thus, the algorithm achieves a two-fold objective – items highly related to "defence" acquire weight even without occurring in the same tuple; and since the weight diffuses as it propagates through the database, a limited form of transitivity is formed.

- *Based on mathematical model of non-linear dynamical systems* - Gibson et al, [1998] suggested that each tuple in the database can be viewed as a set of items and the entire collection of tuples as an abstract set system or hypergraph. According to Zhang et al, [2000] a hypergraph is an extension of a graph such that each hyperedge may be identified by more than two nodes. The node set corresponds to distinct items in the dataset. The STIRR algorithm can be seen as a generalization of the spectral graph partitioning method to the problem of clustering collection of sets (hypergraphs). This generalization involves changes in the algorithms, in particular, the eigen vectors concept is replaced by certain types of non-linear dynamical systems.

- The authors argued that this introduction of dynamical systems is perhaps the most natural way to extend the power of spectral methods to the problem of clustering collections of sets; and authors showed that this approach suggests a framework for analyzing co-occurrence in categorical datasets in a way that avoids many of the pitfalls encountered with intractable combinatorial formulations of the problem [Gibson et al, 1998].

Algorithm and Analysis

Step 1

The Table 3.2 views mine as a relational table with three fields- Groupname, Target and Weapon, each of which can assume one of many possible values. To represent each distinct value as a node, the dataset is viewed as a set T of tuples and each tuple consists of one node from each field. The dataset can be viewed as shown in Table 3.3.

Step 2

To maintain a configuration of distinct nodes as a vector, a weight w_v is assigned to each node v. The configuration is denoted by the letter w.

For the above example

$w' =$ [Node1 Node2 Node3 Node4 Node5 Node6 Node7 Node8 Node9]

where w' is the transpose of w.

Table 3.2: Example Relational Table with Three Fields

Groupname	Target	Weapon
17N	Unknown	Explosives
AKSh	Government	Firearms
.....	.....	.....
....	.....	.....
ASG	Private Citizens & Property	Firearms
ASG	Private Citizens & Property	Explosives

Table 3.3: Dataset View of Table 3.2

Node 1	Node 4	Node 7
Node 2	Node 5	Node 8
....	....	....
....	....	....
Node 3	Node 6	Node 8
Node 3	Node 6	Node 9

Step 3

Initialize the configuration with initial weights. If all distinct values are to be treated equally, then initial configuration weights are assigned as 1. If some nodes are to be favored or diminished, then, that specific nodes can be initialized accordingly.

Step 4

Update the weight w_v of each node v.

1. For each node v, obtain tuples where v occurs.
2. For each tuple $t = \{v, u_1, u_2,..... u_{k-1}\}$ containing v do

    $x = u_1 + u_2 + ... u_{k-1}$

$$w_v = \Sigma\, x$$

e.g. For nodes in example below (initial weights are in parentheses).

Table 3.4: Initial Configuration

Groupname	Target	Weapon
17N (1)	Unknown (1)	Explosives (1)
ASG (1)	Private Citizens & Property (1)	Firearms (1)
ASG (1)	Private Citizens & Property (1)	Explosives (1)

After 1st iteration of STIRR algorithm the values Table 3.4 are modified as shown in Table 3.5

Table 3.5: Result of STIRR Algorithm After First Iteration

Groupname	Target	Weapon
17N (2)	Unknown (2)	Explosives (4)
ASG (4)	Private Citizens & Property (4)	Firearms (2)
ASG (4)	Private Citizens & Property (4)	Explosives (4)

Step 5

Normalize weights obtained of each field separately to eliminate influence of highly occurring values.

Table 3.6: Result of Normalized Weights

Groupname	Target	Weapon
17N (2)	Unknown (2)	Explosives (4)
ASG (4)	Private Citizens & Property (4)	Firearms (2)
ASG (4)	Private Citizens & Property (4)	Explosives (4)

Table 3.7 is obtained after normalization from Table 3.6

Table 3.7: Result of Normalization of Table 3.6

Groupname	Target	Weapon
17N (0.33)	Unknown (0.33)	Explosives (0.67)
ASG (0.67)	Private Citizens & Property (0.67)	Firearms (0.33)
ASG (0.67)	Private Citizens & Property (0.67)	Explosives (0.67)

Step 6

Replace the weights in the old configuration with these normalized weights. A new configuration can be received as follows.

w'= [Node1(0.33) Node2(0.67) Node3(0.33) Node4(0.67) Node5(0.67) Node6(0.33)]

Step 7

Keep iterating Step 1 to Step 6 until the new configuration and the old configuration do not differ (norm of the residual must reach a threshold) and the number of iterations depends on the dataset.

Step 8

The final configuration has weights corresponding to each distinct value in the database (node). This determines which cluster the node belongs to.

Final configuration is w = [0.004 0.048 0.034 0.045 0.003 0.043]

In the example, the first two weights 0.004 and 0.048 correspond to two groups (17N and ASG). If the weights are similar, then they belong to the same cluster. Similarity can be gauged based upon all the resulting weights that obtain and then determining ranges of weights falling in each cluster and weights in the same cluster are deemed to be similar.

The reasons behind choosing the STIRR algorithm for the study are listed below:

- **No apriori quantization:** The format of input dataset is not converted into a numerical format as which was converted in the previous numerical algorithms. This preserves the inherent structure of data and this also avoids problems with sparsely distributed data.

- **Differing from association rules:** Similarity should also be propagated among items in the database that don't occur in the same tuple. Similarity in STIRR is measured purely on co-occurrence. This promotes relationships even among data items that do not occur in the same tuple. STIRR also promotes transitive similarity. If A is related to B and B is related to C, then A is related to C.

- **New Hypergraph approach:** STIRR generalizes the spectral graph partitioning technique into a system based on non-linear dynamical systems. This avoids NP-complete combinatorial formulations that earlier techniques followed.

Apart from many advantages of STIRR, it has the following limitations:

- Does not converge for some input – For some input, the STIRR algorithm fails to converge and it goes on looping and does not reach an end point.

- The algorithm normalizes weights belonging to each attribute separately. This favors attributes that have few distinct values in their domain. These weights tend to obtain higher weights than those attributes that have more distinct values in their domains.

These disadvantages prompted researchers to come up with a new technique called "modified" STIRR or "revised" STIRR.

To cluster the categorical data, the STIRR based algorithms introduced various approaches in order to tackle the problems. Their performance gives various solutions in respect to the time, power and memory which also improves the quality of the clustering. The comparison Table 3.8 shows that k-modes and its prototypes are scalable on discussing with the datasets. The hierarchical algorithm ROCK is based on the attribute values and its occurrence is examined with number of other attribute values with which it exists. The results are also scalable on comparing with other sampling techniques but the efficiency is less than the k-modes. The STIRR algorithm results have acquired either a positive or negative weight on two clusters. In resulting stage, it requires costly post-processing steps. The different partitions of their data set which leads to the conclusion but those clustering must be in meaningful order. The best thing in STIRR algorithm is it converges quickly and identifies clusters in the presence of irrelevant values.

The K-modes algorithm requires more memory operation and also it is applicable for large inputs. For a large dataset, the STIRR needs one pass over the data set and a linear number of in-memory operations. ROCK is not suitable for large datasets and does not contain common quality measure. The above mentioned three algorithms face some disadvantages like text clustering, similarity analyses in clustering tuples and are not able to produce more than two clusters of attribute values. Moreover, the comparison of three algorithms based on single dataset is too difficult. Hence, based on the above observation, fuzzy based algorithm has been proposed in which the result belongs to a single cluster [Jagatheesan S.M and Thiagarasu V, 2014].

Table 3.8: Comparison of Clustering Methods

Clustering Methods				
Algorithms	**Input Parameters**	**Optimized For**	**Outlier Handling**	**Computational Complexity (number of in-memory operations)**
k-modes	Number of cluster	Data Sets with Well-separated Clusters	No	$\varphi(n)$
ROCK	Number of Cluster, Similarity Threshold	Small Data Sets with Noise	Yes	$\varphi(n^2 + nm_m m_a + n^2 \log n)$
STIRR	Initial Configuration, Combining Operator, Stopping Criteria	Large Data Sets with Well separated Clusters	No	$\varphi(n)$

Summary

The k-mode algorithm is not applicable for processing wide range of input which is a major limitation and also it requires in-memory operations. When considering the STIRR algorithm, only one data set can pass over and it also requires a linear number of in-memory for processing large dataset operations. The ROCK algorithm is still in lack of efficiency in determining the quality of the similarity measures. In addition, the limitations such as inefficiency on text clustering, similarity analyses and inability to produce more than two clusters of attribute values are to be explored.

Analyzing the problem of text clustering like language variability where the same meaning can be phrased in various ways. While matching the similarity, the shorter sentences are less effective. Generally, the text clustering which is mainly focused on reducing dimensionality, removing irrelevant data,increasing learning accuracy and improving result comprehensibility. The high dimensional vector space in which every aspect corresponds to a unique keyword and the problem of extracting representative sentences from text is also not effective.

The hierarchical clustering yields better quality clusters than the partitioned methods which are preferred often because of their linear time complexity. Frequent term-based clustering methods are shown to be a promising approach for high dimensionality clustering. A frequent item-based approach of clustering is promising because it provides a natural way of reducing the large dimensionality of the document vector space. The Apriori algorithm is a well-known method for computing frequent term sets in a database. Although the FP-growth algorithm is efficient, sometimes, it is infeasible to construct a main memory-based FP-tree when the database is large which is very common for the case of document clustering. Contents present in text documents contain hierarchical structure and there are many terms present in the documents which are related to more than one theme hence HFRECCA can be useful algorithm for natural language documents.

Generally, the text clustering mainly focuses on reducing dimensionality, removing irrelevant data, increasing learning accuracy and improving result comprehensibility. The solution produced by the existing algorithms like STIRR, ROCK and k-modes are not effective on above mentioned problems. The high dimensional vector space in which every aspect corresponds to a unique keyword and the problem of extracting representative sentences from text is also not effective.

The techniques such as ROCK, STIRR, Modified STIRR and K-modes are analyzed for implementing the categorical data clustering. ROCK not only generates better quality clusters than traditional algorithms but also exhibits good scalability properties. STIRR uses a weight propagation scheme which is viewed as a type of non-linear dynamical system derived from the table of categorical data. This dynamical system converges very fast typical linear in size of the data. The modified STIRR uses the weight updates and all attributes are normalized together. No separate normalization occurs for each attribute. The k-mean algorithm performs better as compared to hierarchical algorithm and takes less time for execution. But on the other hand, hierarchical algorithm provides good quality of results corresponding to k-mean. K-modes is an extension of K-means clustering algorithm, but the working principle of both is same. Instead of means, the concept of modes is used in k-modes algorithm.

Review Questions

1. What is clustering?
2. Briefly explain any three frequent term based text clustering.
3. Explain about the sentence level clustering.
4. Compare the k-means with k-modes method in text clustering.
5. Describe about the ROCK algorithm.
6. Discuss about the STIRR algorithm.

CHAPTER 4

FUZZY BASED MODELING

4.1. Introduction

The fuzzy logic provides a powerful way to categorize a concept in an abstract way by introducing ambiguity and on the other hand, data mining methods are capable of extracting patterns automatically from a large amount of data. The integration of fuzzy logic with data mining methods helps to create more abstract patterns at a higher level than at the data level. Information retrieval and data mining are the two components of the search of information and knowledge extraction from large amounts of data, very large databases or data warehouses. In information retrieval, the user knows approximately what he looks for. For instance, to find an answer to a question or documents corresponding to a given requirement in a database, the user gives a query for the content to be retrieved.

The search is performed in text, multimedia documents or in web pages and trans-media information retrieval takes advantage of the existence of several media to focus on a more specific piece of information, for instance using sound and speech that help in retrieving sequences in a video. The main difficulty lies in the identification of relevant information, i.e. the closest or the most similar to the user's need or expectation. The concept of relevance is very difficult to deal with, mainly because it is strongly dependent on the context of the search and the purpose of the action launched on the basis of such expected relevant information. Asking the user to elicit what he looks for is not an easy task and the more flexible the query-answer process, the more efficient the retrieval. This is a first reason to use fuzzy sets in knowledge representation to enable the user to express his expectations in a language not far from natural. The second reason lies in the approximate matching between the user's queries and existing elements in the database, on the basis of similarities and degrees of satisfaction.

In data mining, the user looks for new knowledge such as relations between variables or general rules for instance and the search is performed in databases or data warehouses. The purpose is to find homogeneous categories, prototypical behaviours, general associations, important features for the recognition of a class of data. In this case, using fuzzy sets bring flexibility in knowledge representation, interpretability in the obtained results, in rules or in characterizations of prototypes. Looking for too strict a relation between variables may be impossible because of the variability of descriptions in the database, while looking for an imprecise relation between variables or to a crisp relation between approximate values of variables may lead to a solution [Bernadette Bouchon-Meunier, 2007; Marie-Jeanne Lesot and Bernadette Bouchon-Meunier, 2004 and Evan Heit, 1997]. The expressiveness of fuzzy rules or fuzzy values of attributes in a simplified natural language is a major quality for the interaction with the final user.

The notion of similarity or more generally of comparison measures is central for all real-world applications and similarity aims at quantifying the extent to which two objects are similar or dissimilar, one to another, providing a numerical value for the comparison. Similarities and dissimilarities between objects are generally evaluated from values of their attributes or variables characterizing these objects. It is the case in various domains such as statistics and data analysis, psychology and pattern recognition for instance. Dissimilarities are classically defined from distances. Similarities and dissimilarities are often expressed from each other: the more similar two objects are, the less dissimilar they are and the smaller their distance. Weights can be associated with variables, according to the semantics of the application or the importance of the variables. It appears that some quantities are used in various environments, with different forms, based on the same principles.

4.2. Fuzzy Machine Learning

Machine learning is an important way to extract knowledge from sets of cases, especially in large scale databases. In this section, the fuzzy machine learning methods are described leaving aside other techniques as for instance fuzzy case based reasoning or fuzzy association rules [Eyke Hullermeier, 2005]. Three methods are successively considered: fuzzy decision trees, fuzzy prototypes and fuzzy clustering. The first two belongs to the supervised learning framework, i.e. they consider that each data point is associated with a category and Fuzzy clustering belongs to the unsupervised learning framework [Bernadette Bouchon-Meunier et al., 2007].

4.2.1. Fuzzy Decision Trees

In classical decision trees, an instance can be associated with only one branch of the tree. Fuzzy Decision Trees (FDT) may simultaneously assign more than one branch to the same instance with gradual certainty. Fuzzy decision trees are particularly interesting for data mining and information retrieval because they enable the user to take into account imprecise descriptions of the cases or heterogeneous values (symbolic, numerical or fuzzy) [Sushmita Mitra et al., 2002; Bernadette Bouchon-Meunier and Christophe Marsala, 2005]. Moreover, they are appreciated for their interpretability, because they provide a linguistic description of the relations between descriptions of the cases and decision to make or class to assign.

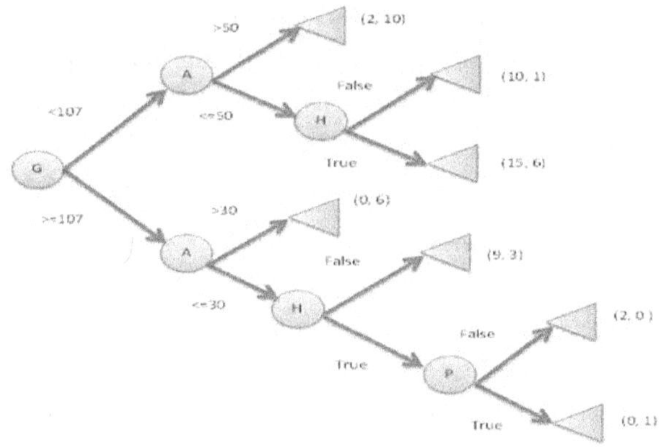

Figure 4.1: Illustration of Decision Tree

The rules obtained through FDT make it easier for the user to interact with the system or the expert to understand, confirm or amend his own knowledge. Another quality of FDT is their robustness, since a small variation of descriptions does not drastically change the decision or the class associated with a case which guarantees a resistance to measurement errors and avoids sharp differences for close values of the descriptions. For these reasons, FDT have been extensively used in the past years. What FDT mainly provide for knowledge extraction is, first a ranking of attributes bringing information about the importance of various criteria in the assignment of decision or class, secondly rules establishing a link between descriptions and decision. Most algorithms to construct decision trees proceed in the same way, the so-called Top Down Induction of Decision Tree (TDIDT) method. They build a tree from the root to the leaves. By successive partitioning of the training set into subsets. Each partition is done by means of a test on an attribute and leads to the definition of a node of the tree. Figure 4.1 illustrate the decision tree.

FDTs preserve the symbolic structure of the tree and its comprehensibility. Nevertheless, FDT can represent concepts with graduated characteristics by producing real-valued outputs with gradual shifts. Janikow [1998] presented a complete framework for building a fuzzy tree including several inference procedures based on conflict resolution in rule-based systems and efficient approximate reasoning methods. Olaru and Wehenkel [2003] presented a new fuzzy decision tree called as Soft Decision Trees (SDT) and this approach combines tree growing and pruning, to determine the structure of the soft decision tree, with refitting and backfitting, to improve its generalization capabilities. They empirically showed that soft decision trees are significantly more accurate than standard decision trees. Moreover, a global model variance study shows a much lower variance for soft decision tree than for standard tree as a direct cause of the improved accuracy. Peng [2004] has used FDT to improve the performance of the classical inductive learning approach in manufacturing processes and proposed a soft discretization of continuous-valued attributes. It has been shown that FDT can deal with the noise or uncertainties existing in the data collected in industrial systems.

Discrimination measure (H) makes it possible to order the attributes according to an increasing accuracy when splitting the training set and the discriminating power of each attribute is valued with regard to the classes. The attribute with the highest discriminating power is selected to construct a node in the decision tree. Methods to construct decision trees, whether crisp or fuzzy, differ mainly in their choice of H; in the fuzzy case, two main families can be distinguished. The first one deals with methods based on generalized entropy: the entropy of fuzzy events as a measure of discrimination. It corresponds to the entropy extended to fuzzy events by substituting probabilities of fuzzy events to classic probabilities. The second one deals with methods based on another family of fuzzy measures, namely a measure of classification ambiguity, defined from both a measure of fuzzy subset hood and a measure of non-specificity. This system implements the previous tree learning method in a flexible framework, allowing the user to choose the measure of discrimination among the previous possibilities, as well as the splitting strategy and the stopping criterion. Furthermore, it offers an internal method for the construction of fuzzy values.

Decision Trees Inducers for Large Datasets

With the recent growth in the amount of data collected by information systems, there is a need for decision trees that can handle large datasets. Catlett [1991] had examined two methods for efficiently growing decision trees from a large database by reducing the computation complexity required for induction. However, the Catlett method requires that all data will be loaded into the main memory before induction. That is to say, the largest dataset that can be induced is bounded by the memory size. Fifield [1992] suggested parallel implementation of the ID3 Algorithm. However, like Catlett, it assumes that all dataset can fit in the main memory. Chan and Stolfo [1997] suggested partitioning the datasets into several disjointed datasets so that each dataset is loaded separately into the memory and used to induce a decision tree. The decision trees are then combined to create a single classifier. However, the experimental results indicated that partition may reduce the classification performance. Classification accuracy of the combined decision trees is not as good as the accuracy of a single decision tree induced from the entire dataset.

The SLIQ (Supervised Learning In Quest) algorithm [Mehta et al., 1996] does not require loading the entire dataset into the main memory; instead it uses a secondary memory (disk). In other words, a certain instance is not necessarily resident in the main memory all the time and it creates a single decision tree from the entire dataset. However, this method also has an upper limit for the largest dataset that can be processed, because it uses a data structure that scales with the dataset size and this data structure must be resident in main memory all the time.

The SPRINT(Serial PaRallelizable INduction of decision Trees) algorithm uses a similar approach [Shafer et al., 1996] and this algorithm induces decision trees relatively quickly and removes all of the memory restrictions from decision tree induction and it scales any impurity based split criteria for large datasets. Gehrke et al., [2000] introduced RainForest; a unifying framework for decision tree classifiers that are capable of scaling any specific algorithms. In addition to its generality, RainForest improves SPRINT by a factor of three. In contrast to SPRINT, however, RainForest requires a certain minimum amount of main memory, proportional to the set of distinct values in a column of the input relation. However, this requirement is considered modest and reasonable. Various decision tree inducers for large datasets can be found in the literature [Alsabti et al., 1998; Freitas and Lavington, 1998; Gehrke et al., 1999].

4.2.2. *Fuzzy Prototype*

Fuzzy prototypes constitute another approach to the characterization of data categories: they provide descriptions or interpretable summarizations of data sets so as to help a user to better apprehend their contents. A prototype is an element chosen to represent a group of data, to summarize it and underline its most characteristic features. It can be defined from a statistic point of view, for instance as the data mean or the median; more complex representatives can also be used, as the Most Typical Value for instance. The prototype notion was also studied from a cognitive science point of view and specific properties were pointed out. It was shown that a prototype not only underlines the common features of the category members, but also their distinctive features as opposed to other categories underlining the specificity of the group.

Furthermore, prototypes were related to the typicality notion, i.e. the fact that all data do not have the same status as regards the group, some members of the group are better examples, more representative or more characteristic than others. It was also shown that the typicality of a point depends both on its resemblance to other members of the group (internal resemblance) and on its dissimilarity to members of other groups (external dissimilarity). These definitions were exploited by Rifqi [1996] who proposed a construction method implementing these principles and exploiting the similarity measure. More precisely, the method consists in first computing internal resemblance and external dissimilarity for each data point, They are respectively defined as the aggregation (mean or median) of the resemblance to the other members of the group and as the aggregation of the dissimilarity to members of other groups, for a given choice of the resemblance and dissimilarity measures.

A typicality degree is computed for each data point as the aggregation of its internal resemblance and external dissimilarity. In a last step, the prototype itself is defined, as the aggregation of the most typical category members. Fuzzy prototypes are defined as the application to fuzzy data or to crisp data that are aggregated into fuzzy sets. Now, the aggregation step that builds prototypes from the most typical data that can build a fuzzy set, derived from the typicality degree distribution. Such fuzzy prototypes then characterize data sets, underlining both the common features of the group members and their distinctive features and modeling their un-sharp boundaries.

4.2.3. Fuzzy Clustering

Fuzzy clustering methods have the potential to manage the situations efficiently. Conventional clustering means classifying the given observation as exclusive subsets (clusters). That is, it can be seen clearly whether an object belongs to a cluster or not. However, such a partition is insufficient to represent many real situations. Therefore, a fuzzy clustering method is offered to construct clusters with uncertain boundaries. Hence, this method allows that one object belongs to some overlapping clusters to some degree. In other words, the essence of fuzzy clustering is to consider not only the belonging status to the clusters, but also to consider to what degree do the objects belong to the clusters [Mika Sato-Ilic and Lakhmi C. Jain, 2006].

Contrary to fuzzy decision trees and fuzzy prototype construction methods, clustering algorithms belong to the unsupervised learning framework, i.e. they do not consider that a decomposition of the data set into categories is available. They perform data mining as the identification of relevant subgroups of the data, determining subsets of similar data and thus highlighting the underlying structure of the data set. More precisely relevant subgroups are such that points within a group are more similar to one another than points assigned to a different subgroup. Thus, as the previous learning methods such as Fuzzy decision trees, Fuzzy prototype and Fuzzy clustering, they rely on comparison measures.

The clustering aim can also be expressed as the decomposition of the data set into subgroups that are both homogeneous and distinct: the fact that clusters are homogeneous implies that points in the same subgroup indeed resemble one another which justifies their grouping. The fact that they are distinct justifies the individual existence of each cluster that captures different characteristics of the data. Through this decomposition, clustering leads to a simplified representation of the data set that can be summarized by a reduced number of clusters instead of considering each individual data point.

The fuzzy set theory proves its advantage in the framework through the notion of membership degrees: in crisp clustering algorithms such as the k-means or hierarchical methods, a point is assigned to a single cluster. Now this is not adapted to the frequent case where clusters overlap and points have partial memberships to several subgroups. The first fuzzy clustering algorithm called fuzzy c-means that was generalized by Bezdek [1984]. Since then, many variants have been proposed to address specific aims adapting to other data or cluster types [Frank Klawonn and Frank Hoppener, 2009; Daoqiang Zhang and Songcan Chen, 2002] or considering fuzzy clustering at a more formal level leading to the vast fuzzy clustering domain.

Fuzzy clustering is a partition based clustering scheme and is particularly useful when there are no apparent clear groupings in the data set. Partitioning schemes provide automatic detection of cluster boundaries and in case of fuzzy clustering, these cluster boundaries overlap. Every individual data entity (a conformer, in this case) belongs to not one but all the clusters with varying degrees of membership. It is also important to understand the difference between unsupervised classification and supervised classification. In supervised classification, a collection of *labeled* (preclassified) patterns is provided; the problem is to label a newly encountered, yet unlabeled pattern. Typically, the given labeled (*training*) patterns are used to learn the descriptions of classes which in turn are used to label a new pattern.

In the case of clustering, the problem is to group a given collection of unlabeled patterns into meaningful clusters. In a sense, labels are associated with clusters also, but these category labels are *data driven*; that is, they are obtained solely from the data. Clustering is useful in several exploratory pattern-analysis, grouping, decision-making, and machine-learning situations, including data mining, document retrieval, image segmentation, and pattern classification.

However, in many such problems, there is little prior information (e.g., statistical models) available about the data and the decision-maker must make a few assumptions about the data as much as possible. It is under these restrictions that clustering methodology is particularly appropriate for the exploration of interrelationships among the data points to make an assessment (perhaps preliminary) of their structure [Zoubin, 2004].

4.3.   Fuzzy Logic

In 1965, Professor L.A. Zadeh of the University of California, Berkely outlined fuzzy theory and introduced fuzzy set theory and operation, fuzzy logic based controller, etc., In 1970, fuzzy logic theory was applied in many systems in Japan, China and Europe. In 1987, sixteen station subway railway systems were built and it worked with a fuzzy logic-based automatic train operation control system in Sendai and Japan. It was proved that by applying fuzzy logic based automation, the train ride was smooth. Fuzzy logic is a powerful problem-solving methodology and it has myriad of applications in embedded information processing and control. Fuzzy provides remarkably simple and definite conclusions. Conclusions are made from vague, ambiguous and imprecise information. Fuzzy logic resembles human decision making and it has ability to work from approximate data and also it finds precise solutions. Classical logic requires a deep understanding of a system, exact equations and precise numeric values. Fuzzy logic provides an alternative way of thinking and fuzzy logic allows modeling complex systems while using a higher level of abstraction that originates from knowledge and experience. Fuzzy logic expresses knowledge with subjective concepts like bright red, very hot, long time, very quick etc. are mapped into exact numeric ranges.

Fuzzy Logic is an extension of Boolean logic and it incorporates partial values of truth. Instead of sentences being "Completely True" or "Completely False". In fuzzy logic, they are assigned a value which represents their degree of truthiness. In fuzzy systems, values are indicated by a number called as truth value and it lies in the range from 0 to 1.0. 0 represents absolute falseness and 1.0 represents absolute truth. Fuzzification is generalization of theory from discrete to continuous. Fuzzy logic allows computers to answer 'to a certain degree' unlike Boolean logic (one extreme or the other). Computers are allowed to think more 'human-like'. However, it is true only to a certain degree. In fuzzy logic, machines think in degrees and it can solve problems in the cases where there is no simple mathematical model and it solves highly non-linear processes. Fuzzy logic uses expert knowledge to make decisions and a block diagram of fuzzy logic system is shown in Figure 4.2.

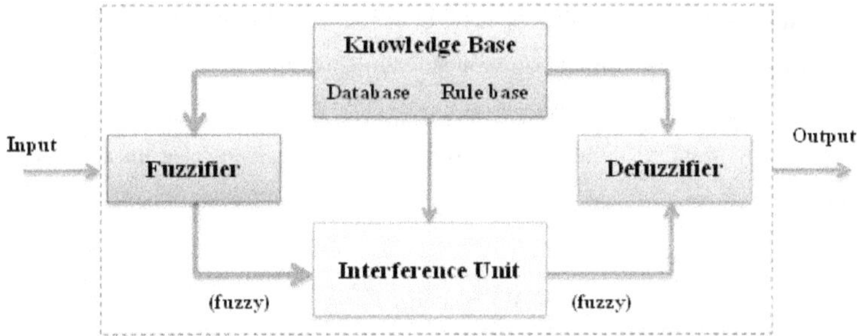

Figure 4.2: Block Diagram of Fuzzy Logic System

Fuzzy logic was first invented as a representation scheme and it acts as calculus for uncertain or vague notions and also it allows more human-like interpretations. Fuzzy logic has put reasoning in machines by resolving intermediate categories between notations like true/false, hot/cold etc. Fuzzy logic is a problem-solving control system methodology. It lends itself to implementation in systems ranging from small, simple, embedded micro-controllers to large, multi-channel, networked PC or workstation-based data acquisition control systems etc. It can be implemented in software, hardware or a combination of both. Fuzzy logic provides a simple way to arrive at a definite conclusion. Conclusion is based upon ambiguous or vague, noisy, imprecise or missing input information. Fuzzy logic's approach to control problems simply mimics how a person will make efficient decisions much faster.

Principles of Fuzzy logic

The step for designing a simple fuzzy logic control system is as follows:

- Identify the variables (Input, states and output) of the plant.
- Partition the universe of discourse or the interval spanned by each variable into a number of fuzzy subsets, assigning each a linguistic labels (subset includes all the elements in the universe).
- Assign or determine a membership function for each fuzzy subset.
- Assign the fuzzy relationship between the "inputs" or the "states" fuzzy subsets on the one hand and the "output" fuzzy subsets on the other hand, thus forming the rule base.
- Choose appropriate scaling factor for the input and variables in order to normalize the variable to the [0,1] or [-1,1] interval.

- Fuzzy inputs to the controller.
- Use fuzzy appropriate reasoning to input the output contributed from each rule.
- Aggregate the fuzzy outputs recommended by each rule.
- Apply defuzzification to form a crisp output.

It is quite important to define the control objectives and control criteria by answering the following questions.

- What is to be controlled?
- What has to be done to control the system?
- What kind of response should be there?
- What are the possible failure modes in the systems?

It is necessary to determine the input and output relationships. A minimum number of variables are chosen for input to the fuzzy logic inference engine typically error and rate-of-change-of-error. Using the rule-based structure of fuzzy logic, the control problem is broken down into a series of IF X AND Y THEN Z rules. Rules must define the desired system output response for the given system input conditions. Number and complexity of rules depends on the number of input parameters be processed. It also depends upon the number fuzzy variables associated with each parameter and it is preferred to use at least one variable and its time derivative. A single instantaneous error parameter should be used along with its rate of change. Fuzzy logic membership functions need to be created which define the meaning (values) of input/output terms that are used in the rules. System need to be tested, evaluated for results. Tune the rules and membership functions, until satisfactory results are obtained, retest the system.

4.4. Fuzzy Inference System

Fuzzy Inference Systems (FIS) are rule-based systems and it is based on fuzzy set theory and fuzzy logic. FIS are mappings from an input space to an output space and it allows constructing structures which are used to generate responses (outputs) for certain stimulations (inputs). Response of FIS is based on stored knowledge (relationships between responses and stimulations). Knowledge is stored in the form of a rule base and rule base is a set of rules. Rule base expresses relations between inputs of system and its' expected outputs and knowledge is obtained by eliciting information from specialists. These systems are usually known as fuzzy expert systems. Another common denomination for FIS is fuzzy knowledge-based systems and it is also called as data-driven fuzzy systems.

Fuzzy inference is the process of formulating the mapping from a given input to an output using fuzzy logic. The mapping then provides a basis from which decisions can be made, or patterns discerned. The process of fuzzy inference involves all of the pieces that are described in the previous sections: membership functions, fuzzy logic operators and if-then rules. There are two types of fuzzy inference systems that can be implemented in the Fuzzy Logic Toolbox: Mamdani-type and Sugeno-type. These two types of inference systems vary somewhat in the way outputs are determined.

Fuzzy Inference Engine

Fuzzy Inference Systems are conceptually very simple. They consist of an input, a processing, and an output stage [M. Blej and M.Azizi, 2016]. The input stage receives inputs like deadline, execution time, laxity and so on, and maps these to appropriate membership functions and truth values. In the processing stage, each specific rule is invoked and the corresponding result is generated. Then results are combined so that it will be given as an input to the output stage. In output stage, the combined result is converted back into a specific value [L.X. Wang, 1996]. The membership function of a fuzzy set is a generalization of the indicator function in classical sets. In fuzzy logic, it represents the degree of truth as an extension of valuation. It can be expressed in the form of a curve that defines how each point in the input space is mapped to a membership value (or degree of membership) between 0 and 1. It can also have many forms (triangular, trapezoidal and Bell curves). The processing stage also called inference engine is based on a set of logical rules in the form of IF-THEN statements. An example of fuzzy IF-THEN rules is: IF Speed is "Low" AND Race is "Dry" THEN Braking is "Soft", Where the IF part is called the "antecedent" and the THEN part is called the "consequent". The terms Speed, Race and Braking are linguistic variables, and Low, Dry and Soft are linguistic terms. Each linguistic term corresponds to a value of the membership function. Typically, Fuzzy Inference Systems have dozens of rules [H. Deldari, M. A.,2006]. The inference engine processes the inputs and generates outputs based on the rules already defined. There are five steps in the fuzzy inference: Fuzzify inputs, Apply the fuzzy operator, Apply the implication method, Aggregate all outputs, Defuzzify outputs. Below is a brief overview of these five steps. The first step is to take the inputs and determine the degree to which they belong to each of the appropriate fuzzy sets via membership functions. Fuzzification of the input amounts to either a table lookup or a function evaluation. After fuzzifying the inputs, one can know then the degree to which each part of the antecedent has been fullfilled for each rule. So if the antecedent of a given rule has more than one part, the fuzzy operator is applied to obtain one number that represents the result of the antecedent for that rule. This number will then be applied to the output function. The number of inputs to the fuzzy operator is two or more membership values from fuzzified input variables. Whereas the output is a single truth value. The output fuzzy set has been modified by the implication function to the degree specified by the antecedent. Since decisions are based on the testing of all of the rules in the Fuzzy Inference Subsystem (FIS), the results from each rule must be combined in order to generate the final decision. Aggregation is the process by which the fuzzy sets that represent the outputs of each rule are combined into a single fuzzy set. It occurs only once for each output variable, just prior to the fifth and final step, defuzzification. The input for the defuzzification process is an aggregate output fuzzy set, and the output is a single number [M. Sabeghi and Mahmoud Naghibzadeh, 2006]. At runtime, based on the parameter of tasks, the fuzzy scheduler selects the task with the highest priority that is ready for execution. Several parameters determine the priority of tasks: task deadline, task criticality, task execution time, laxity. The task deadline is the time before the task should be completed. The task criticality relates to the consequences of missing a deadline. The worst case execution time of task is his execution time. Laxity is the time that separates the task deadline and the worst case execution time of task. These parameters constitute the linguistic variables and then fuzzified. Fuzzy rules are then applied to the linguistic variables to compute the service value. The linguistic values for the chosen parameters are defined. There are two common inference methods: Mamdani's fuzzy inference method proposed in 1975 by Ebrahim Mamdani [Mamdani et al., 1975] and Takagi-Sugeno-Kang, method of fuzzy inference introduced in 1985 [M. Sugeno, 1985]. In the following section and these two methods are presented with comparative study.

Mamdani-type FIS vs. Sugeno-Type FIS

Mamdani method is widely accepted for capturing expert knowledge. It allows us to describe the expertise in more intuitive, more human-like manner. However, Mamdani-type FIS entails a substantial computational burden. On the other hand, Sugeno method is computationally efficient and works well with optimization and adaptive techniques, which makes it very attractive in control problems, particularly for dynamic non linear systems. These adaptive techniques can be used to customize the membership functions so that fuzzy system best models the data. The most fundamental difference between Mamdani-type FIS and Sugeno-type FIS is the way the crisp output is generated from the fuzzy inputs. While Mamdani-type FIS uses the technique of defuzzification of a fuzzy output, Sugeno-type FIS uses weighted average to compute the crisp output. The expressive power and interpretability of Mamdani output is lost in the Sugeno FIS since the consequents of the rules are not fuzzy [A. Haman and N. D. Geogranas, 2008]. But Sugeno has better processing time since the weighted average replace the time consuming defuzzification process. Due to the interpretable and intuitive nature of the rule base, Mamdani-type FIS is widely used in particular for decision support application. Other differences are that Mamdani FIS has output membership functions whereas Sugeno FIS has no output membership functions. Mamdani FIS is less flexible in system design in comparison to Sugeno FIS as latter can be integrated with ANFIS tool to optimize the outputs.

FIS are usually divided into two categories viz. Multiple Input and Multiple Output (MIMO) systems and Multiple Input and Single Output (MISO) systems. The MIMO systems return several outputs based on the inputs which it receives.

MISO systems are those where only one output is returned from multiple inputs. MIMO systems are decomposed into a set of MISO systems which work in parallel. In terms of inference process, there are two main classes of FIS viz. the Mamdani-type FIS and the Takagi-Sugeno-Kang (TSK) type FIS and TSK FIS is also called as Sugeno FIS [Abraham, A, 2001; Gorriz, J.M, 2009]

Comparison of Sugeno Type FIS and Mamdani-type FIS

Both Sugeno and Mamdani FIS can be used to perform the similar tasks. Rule base and fuzzification remain the same for the variables. There are various defuzzifiers that can be chosen for a Mamdani FIS and these defuzzifiers also originate similar results in a Sugeno FIS and there is a certain overlap between both types of systems. Mamdani FIS is more widely used and it is used for decision support applications because of its intuitive and interpretable nature. Consequents of the rules in a Sugeno FIS do not have a direct semantic mean. This means that they are not linguistic terms. Also, this interpretability is partially lost. Sugeno FIS rules consequents can have many parameters per rule as per input values.

4.5.   Fuzzy Clustering Techniques

The process-data modelling technique uses fuzzy logic and statistical clustering. Patterns of system calls must be represented as a model of normal behaviour. The fuzzy model should extract the essence of correctness or normalness of a process. Clustering methods group data by centers and clustering techniques partition data into several clusters in such a way that similar objects belong to the same cluster. The cluster centers represent the most normal of sequences and deviations from the centers indicate behaviour that is more abnormal.

Fuzzy clustering involves fuzzy logic and fuzzy logic defines what degree of normality a classifier should give to new process-data compared against the database. Fuzzy logic can better help represent the uncertainty that lies in the data. Hence, look at various fuzzy clustering techniques that can determine the true nature of the underlying data to help predict whether new sequences are abnormal or not and to what degree.

In fuzzy clustering, each data element belongs to several partitions to certain degrees. Non-fuzzy clustering techniques generate different partitions to which data elements belong and these partitions are disjoint. In fuzzy clustering, the partitions are not disjoint. Several previous attempts have tried to create a good fuzzy clustering algorithm. A general high level partitioning fuzzy clustering algorithm called Fuzzy Clustering Algorithm (FCA) is presented by Jain, et al., [1999]. Additionally, a generalization of the Fuzzy C-Means (FCM) algorithm was presented by Bezdek[1981], while an adaptive variant for detecting circular and elliptical boundaries was presented by Dave [1992]. These algorithms have failed when trying to work with large data sets and in addition to these algorithms; focus will be on quantitative data.

In order to handle categorical or qualitative data, Ralambondrainy [1995] represented multiple categorical attributes by using binary attributes to indicate the presence or absence of a category. The binary values were then used in the well-known c-means algorithm. The number of binary values becomes very large when each attribute has many categories. The complexity of the binary feature vector technique was reduced in the k-modes algorithm, introduced by Zhexue Huang [1998]. It reduces the complexity by using a simple matching dissimilarity measure and the algorithm is very sensitivities to initialization.

The fuzzy version of the k-modes algorithm was first proposed by Zhexue Huang and Michael K. Ng [1999] as an extension for the fuzzy c-means algorithm. The fuzzy c-means algorithm is the most prominent fuzzy clustering algorithm [Bezdek, J.C. et al., 1984]. The fuzzy k-modes algorithm was developed to cluster large categorical data sets in data mining. They added the element of fuzzy logic to represent better the uncertainty found in the data set.

Unfortunately, the fuzzy k-modes algorithm gets stuck in *local* optima. Several heuristics have been developed to find the *global* optima. One heuristic uses fuzzy centroids instead of the hard-type centroids [Kim, D. W. et al., 2004]. Another variation represents categorical data clusters with k-populations [Kim, D. W. et al., 2005]. Still, another way to find the global optimum is presented by Ng et al., [2002]. The authors used a Tabu search technique and these methods include a random restart method, variable neighbor search, tabu search and candidate list search.

Fuzzy Clustering Validation Techniques

The fuzzy k-modes algorithm has a drawback and one must specify the number of clusters beforehand. To combat this drawback by running the fuzzy k-modes for several cluster sizes and picking the best one according to some criterion. This criterion is known as a validity index. Validity indexes measure the fitness of a partition scheme for a given data set and a validity index shows how closely a certain pre-defined number of clusters fit the underlying data set. Good validity scores indicate that the clusters closely model the underlying truth of nature of the data patterns. To use the validity indexes to determine how many clusters should be used in the process-data model.

Halkidi, et. al. [2001] identified three approaches to investigate cluster validity. *External criteria* use a pre-defined structure for the data set which reflects the intuitive understanding of the data. The results of the clustering algorithm are evaluated against this model. *Internal criteria* use the quantities of the vectors of the data set themselves. *Relative criteria* compare the structures of several clustering schemes together, usually using the same algorithm but with different parameters. The authors later identified two evaluation criteria for the selection of optimal clustering schemes: *compactness* which involves how close the members of a certain cluster are to each other; and *separation* which shows how far apart the clusters are from each other. Fuzzy clustering validity indices seek clustering schemes where the dataset exhibits a high degree of membership in one cluster. Fuzzy validity indices divide into two general categories. One category uses only the membership values of the data sets to all clusters and the second uses both the membership values and the underlying structure of the data set.

Bezdek et al., [1984] first introduced the partition coefficient and the partition entropy coefficient. Although effective, these indices have several drawbacks. The indices tend to decrease or increase monotonically as the number of clusters increase. In these cases, one should take the point of maximum curvature on the graph. On the other hand, one can take the global minima in certain cases where the number of clusters is low, around the square root of the number of unique strings. The other category of fuzzy clustering validation extracts the knowledge of the underlying structure of the data. The indices use distance as well as membership values.

Various indices of this type include the Xie-Beni index [1991], the Fukuyama-Sugeno index and other indices proposed by Gath and Geva [1989], which are based on hyper-volume and density. All these indices use some sort of distance measure to extract the underlying structure of the data.

A newer validity index for fuzzy qualitative data was found. This index does not contain the problems of converting a known quantitative index to a qualitative index. The index is presented by Tsekouras et al., [2004]. The authors tackle the two problems that the fuzzy k-modes algorithm presents: ① its sensitivity to initialization and ② the *a priori* knowledge of the number of clusters. They design a new three step categorical data-clustering algorithm that can determine the proper number of clusters for the fuzzy k-modes algorithm based on an entropy fuzzy clustering method, the fuzzy k-modes algorithm and a new validity index.

Fuzzy logic is a form of many-valued logic; it deals with reasoning that is approximate rather than fixed and exact. Compared to traditional binary sets (where variables may take on true or false values) fuzzy logic variables may have a truth value that ranges in degree between 0 and 1. Fuzzy logic has been extended to handle the concept of partial truth where the truth value may range between completely true and completely false [Pivnickova L et al., 2013]. Furthermore, when linguistic variables are used, these degrees may be managed by specific functions. Irrationality can be described in terms of what is known as the fuzzjective [N Ahlawat. et al., 2014]

Fuzzy clustering relaxes the requirement that data points have to be assigned to one and only one cluster. In these algorithms data points can belong to more than one cluster and even with different levels of membership. These non-exclusive cluster assignments can represent the database structure in a more natural way, especially when clusters do not have a perfect boundary or what is the same, when clusters overlap. At these overlapping boundaries, the fuzzy membership can indicate the ambiguity of the cluster assignment. There are two major approaches to this gradual cluster assignment: the first one is probabilistic methods where one can find the Fuzzy C-Means algorithm among others. The second one is the possibilistic methods where the Possibilistic fuzzy C-Means (PCM) is placed.

FCM: Fuzzy C-Means

This algorithm allows gradual membership which will be measured as degrees in [0,1] and this makes the data model much more detailed and allows the total model to express how ambiguous or definite the database is. Given that now memberships are fuzzy, they cannot be expressed with only one value or label.

Now, they have to be a vector for each point $xi \in X$ the length of which is c, the number of clusters:

$$u_j = (u_{1j} , ..., u_{cj})^T$$

where u_{ij} represents the membership to each cluster.

In this algorithm, all data are equally included and receives the same weight as all other data, although the distribution of this weight among the clusters differs from one object to another. As consequence, no cluster can contain all data and the membership values have to be normalized for each object. Obviously, the closer a data point lies to the center of a cluster, the higher its degree of membership should be to this cluster. The problem of finding the best partition of the data set not only relies in the optimization of a cost index where computed the sum of all distances from the point to their cluster center is computed, but it is also desired to maximize the degrees of a membership.

PCM: Possibilistic Fuzzy C-Means

It is desirable to have the property of the probabilistic membership degrees, although sometimes it can be misleading. High values for the membership of a datum in more than one cluster mean that the point is at the same distance to those clusters. If there is another point with similar characteristics this can suggest that both points are close, but this might not be true. Both points are equally distanced to the two clusters, but they are not close.

The normalization of membership values can lead further to undesired effects in the presence of noise and outliers. The membership values affect the clustering results, since data point weights influence on cluster prototypes. A more intuitive assignment of degrees of membership can be achieved by dropping the normalization constraint, avoiding undesirable normalization effects. This last point can be highly desirable if the clusters are considered completely independent from one another.

The main difference between FCM and PCM is that probabilistic algorithms are forced to partition the data exhaustively while the corresponding possibilistic methods are not compelled to do so. Another difference is that probabilistic methods distribute the total membership of the data points while the possibilistic methods are required to determine the data point weights themselves. Probabilistic algorithms attempt to cover all data points with clusters which can be an advantage when the real clusters have this property. In the possibilistic case, there is no interaction between clusters. Given that the initialization of the PCM is much more complex than the initialization of FCM but it performs better, sometimes FCM is used to initialize ηi and after that the possibilistic algorithm is applied. However, this has a high computational cost and some applications make it impractical.

As the distance measure used is the Euclidean distance only spherical shapes can be detected. Some algorithms have been designed to overcome this problem, by modifying the distance computed. All of them can work with both probabilistic or possibilistic methods [J. Abonyi et al., 2007].

GK: Gustafson-Kessel [Abonyi. J et al., 2007]

This algorithm replaces the Euclidean distance used in FCM and PCM by the Mahalanobis distance, in order to adopt various shapes and sizes of the clusters. In FCM and PCM, as the distance function used is the Euclidean distance, the shapes of the clusters to be identified are only hyper-spherical. GK models each cluster D_i by both its center, c_i and its covariance matrix Σ_i . Both parameters have to be learned and the eigenvalues of the matrix Σ_i represent the shape of the cluster D_i. Specific constraints can be set depending on the requirements of the application.

For instance, restricting to axis-parallel cluster shapes by considering only diagonal matrices. This case is preferred when clustering is used for the generation of fuzzy rule systems and the distance function is now defined as:

$$d_{ij}^2 = (x_j - c_i)^T \sum_i^{-1} (x_j - c_i)$$

Apart from that, the cost function and the update equation for the cluster centers and the update equation for the membership degrees are identical to the FCM or PCM, depending which approach is being used. GK extracts more information about the data than FCM and PCM, but it is more sensitive to its initialization. Then, a good recommendation could be the use of FCM or PCM for its initialization and afterwards, applying GK.

FSC: Fuzzy Shell Clustering [Abonyi. J et al., 2007]

All the algorithms described so far in this section detect shapes like solid objects and thus they are called solid algorithms. Variants of FCM and PCM have been proposed to detect some other shapes like lines, circles or ellipses called as shell algorithms. They extract prototypes that have a different nature from the data points and for that they need to modify the definition of the distance function and some of these algorithms are:

FCV: Fuzzy C-Varieties [Abonyi. J et al., 2007]

It detects lines, planes or hyperplanes and each cluster is a subspace defined by a point and a set of orthogonal unit vectors $D_i = (c_i, e_{i1} \dots e_{iq})$ where q is the dimension of the subspace.

The distance function is now defined as:

$$d(x_j, D_i) = || x_i - c_i ||^2 - \sum_{i=1}^q (x_i - c_i)^T e_{il}$$

This algorithm can also be used for construction of locally linear models of data with underlying interrelations.

FCQS: Fuzzy C-Quadratic Shells [Abonyi. J et al., 2007]

This algorithm is able to recognize ellipses, hyperbolas, parabolas or linear clusters. Sometimes, the projections of the circle-shaped clusters form an ellipse where this algorithm is very useful. Other fuzzy shell algorithms are AFCE to recognize ellipses, FCRS to recognize non-smooth shapes, such as rectangles, FC2RS to recognize rectangles and other non-smooth polygonal shapes.

KFC: Kernel-based Fuzzy Clustering [Abonyi. J et al., 2007]

Kernel learning methods constitute a set of machine learning algorithms that make it possible to extend classic linear algorithms. The kernel variants of fuzzy clustering algorithms further modify the distance function to handle non-vectorial data, such as sequences, trees or graphs, without needing to modify the algorithms themselves. The aim is two-fold: first, they make possible to treat tasks that require a more complex algorithm than a linear one and second, they make it possible to apply algorithms to data that are not described in a vectorial form. More generally, kernel methods can be applied independently of the data nature. Kernel methods are based on an implicit data representation transformation with which the normal space is transformed to feature space. The second principle of kernel methods is that data are not handled directly in the feature space. But they are only handled through their scalar products that are computed by using the initial representation. The algorithms are written only in terms of scalar products between data. Then, the data representation improvement comes from using scalar products based on an implicit transformation of the data.

Applying this approach to clustering, it aims at extracting prototypes that have a different nature from the data points and thus it modifies the concept of distance between points. In the kernel approach, the similarity is computed between pairs of data points and does not involve cluster centres. On the other hand, kernel methods do not have an explicit representative of the cluster and cannot be seen as prototype based clustering methods. The application of kernel methods needs to select the kernel and its parameters and this may be difficult but they are able to cluster a non-vectorial defined object which is one of their advantages.

FCRM: Fuzzy C-Regression Models [Hathaway. RJ and Bezdek. JC, 1993]

Various algorithms are designed, instead to form different groups, to construct a model based on the inputs in order to predict the output from a new input. These algorithms are also called model-based clustering algorithms. FCRM is one of these types which will be better described in below equation. Its cost function basically tries to find a set of fuzzy models to represent the output with a linear combination of the inputs.

Given a data set where each independent input observation x_k has a correspondent output observation y_k, it is assumed that several lineal models c describe the relation between the input and the output: $y^\hat{} = f_i(x; \beta_i) + \in_i$ where $1 \leq i \leq c$ and this is known as a switching regression model. If each object is described by a combination of all or some models, then the problem to solve can be divided into two: finding good estimations of parameters βi which define $y^\hat{}$ (predicted output) and finding the membership of each object to each one of those models.

Basically, the steps to find the solution are:

1. Initialization of the variables: m, $U^{(0)}$, $\in$, etc. Choice of the error measure E_{ik}.
2. Calculate the values for all β_i. This will be done with least squares.
3. Update the membership matrix.
4. Compare the new matrix with the last one, if the sum of changes between the two matrices is smaller than ϱ then iteration will stop. Otherwise, go back to 2.

This algorithm is tested to work very well when the correct number of clusters, c, is chosen and when data is distributed following lineal models.

AFCR: Adaptive Fuzzy Clustering and Fuzzy Prediction Models [Ryoke. M et al., 1995]

This algorithm is based on the FCRM which could also be classified as a model-based algorithm. It addresses the problem of the shapes of the clusters and they are changed dynamically and adaptively in the clustering process. The steps to find the solution are very similar to the case of the FCRM:

1. Initialization of the variables: m, $U^{(0)}$, $\in$, etc. Choice of the error measure E_{ik} and distance measure D_{ik}.
2. Calculate the values for all β_i. This will be done applying least squares using the membership matrix.
3. Update the membership matrix and compute α_i.
4. Compare the new matrix with the last one, if the sum of changes between the two matrices is smaller than $\in$ then iteration will stop. Otherwise, go back to 2.

Summary

Fuzzy logic is a powerful tool for the formulation of expert knowledge and the combination of imprecise information from different sources. To achieve meaningful results, the imprecision in all text information should be taken into account. Further, characterization of clusters indicates the extent to which a cluster is exceptional or representative of the data. The characterization makes it possible to distinguish major trends, typical behaviours and the intuitive descriptions of the models. Consider for instance, a device having three modes, described as "high", "low" and "abnormally low". The exceptional case "abnormally low" is part of the system description which is indeed necessary but the adverb "abnormally" underlines its specificity.

The major challenge is the search or the extraction of information and knowledge from large amounts of data. This research work focuses on how the theory supported the application, ignoring a large set of other difficulties, appearing when dealing with real world challenges: as for instance technical issues, solutions for fast execution (essential in the case of large data sets), management of large data bases etc. In this chapter, the necessity of fuzzy clustering has been highlighted. The importance of fuzzy inference system has been analyzed and the concepts involved in fuzzy inference systems such as fuzzy decision tree and fuzzy prototype have been elaborately discussed in this chapter. The requirement of an efficient fuzzy clustering algorithm for detecting text clusters have been identified and the necessity of modelling Fuzzy based categorical text clustering has also been identified.

Review Questions

1. Write a note on fuzzy decision trees.
2. Briefly discuss about fuzzy clustering.
3. Write down the principles of fuzzy logic.
4. Compare MAMDANI-type with SUGENO type fuzzy inference systems.
5. Describe fuzzy C-means.
6. Discuss about any three fuzzy clustering techniques.

CHAPTER 5

RECENT TRENDS IN FUZZY BASED CLUSTERING ALGORITHM

5.1. Introduction

As considered several approaches in clustering of data based on a certain pattern, the similarities play a vital role in clustering sentences on the prediction in order to produce an efficient result comparing to the previous approaches. Hence, a fuzzy logic based approach has been proposed for finding the similarities to form a cluster, based on the relational prototypes. A semantic clustering and fuzzy based categorical text clustering approach is practiced to bring more accuracy in mining process. The algorithm indentifies the semantically related sentences and avoids duplication on the given data set. The information retrieval based on the proposed algorithm will maximize the accuracy compared to the earlier ones.

5.2. Overview of Fuzzy Categorical Clustering

The fuzzy clustering algorithm that can in principle be applied to any relational clustering problem. But eventually, it depends on the excellence of the dataset and in the case of sentence clustering; this efficiency in performance may be achieved through the sentence similarity measures which may in turn be based on improved word sense disambiguation. This research work further improves the Fuzzy categorical text clustering to reduce the time consumption which was considered as the major limitation on the existing approaches. In text processing, the major part is sentence clustering since sentence clustering is nothing but grouping of sentences which are similar meanings into clusters. Then, the task is performed by applying standard clustering algorithms to group sentences into clusters. Various traditional methods such as STIRR, ROCK and k-Modes are followed in practice that represents the sentences as vectors in term space and applies best clustering algorithm to achieve the result accuracy. A novel sentence clustering scheme has been presented based on fuzzy logic on sentences over the term clusters. The major challenge in implementing the sentence clustering approach is language variability where the same meaning can be phrased in various ways. The shorter the sentences are the less effective becomes exact matching of their terms. Various traditional methods in text processing are mainly focused on reducing dimensionality, removing irrelevant data, increasing learning accuracy and improving result comprehensibility. The embedded methods involves in feature selection which to be a part of training process that are usually meant for learning algorithms. Traditional machine learning algorithms such as decision trees and artificial neural networks are discussed which are all depend on the embedded approaches.

Decision Tree

Decision trees are powerful and popular tools for classification and prediction. The attractiveness of decision trees is due to the fact that, in contrast to neural networks, decision trees represent rules. Rules can readily be expressed so that humans can understand them or even directly used in a database access language so that records falling into a particular category may be retrieved. Decision tree learning is one of the most successful techniques for supervised classification learning. The goal is to create a model that predicts the value of a target variable based on several input variables. Assume that all of the features have finite discrete domains and there is a single target feature called the classification. Each element of the domain of the classification is called a class. A decision tree or a classification tree is a tree in which each internal (non-leaf) node is labeled with an input feature. The arcs coming from a node labeled with a feature are labeled with each of the possible values of the feature. Each leaf of the tree is labeled with a class or a probability distribution over the classes [Rokach, Lior and Maimon, O. 2008]. In data mining, decision trees can be described also as the combination of mathematical and computational techniques to aid the description, categorization and generalization of a given set of data. In some applications, the accuracy of a classification or prediction is the only thing that matters. In some situations, the ability to explain the reason for a decision is crucial.

Artificial Neural Network

Neural networks are of particular interest because they offer a means of efficiently modeling large and complex problems. Neural networks may be used in classification problems or for regressions. An artificial neural network can be defined as an information processing system consisting of many processing elements which are joined together in a structure inspired by the cerebral cortex of the brain. The processing elements considered in the definition of ANN are usually organized in a sequence of layers, with full connections between layers. Typically, there are three (or more) layers: an input layer where data are presented to the network through an input buffer, an output layer with a buffer that holds the output response to a given input and one or more intermediate or hidden layers. (Figure 5.1)

The operation of an artificial neural network involves two processes: learning and recall. Learning is the process of updating the connection weights in response to external stimuli presented at the input buffer. The network "learns" in accordance with a learning rule governing the adjustment of connection weights in response to learning examples applied at the input and output buffers. Recall is the process of accepting an input and producing a response determined by the geometry and synaptic weights of the network.

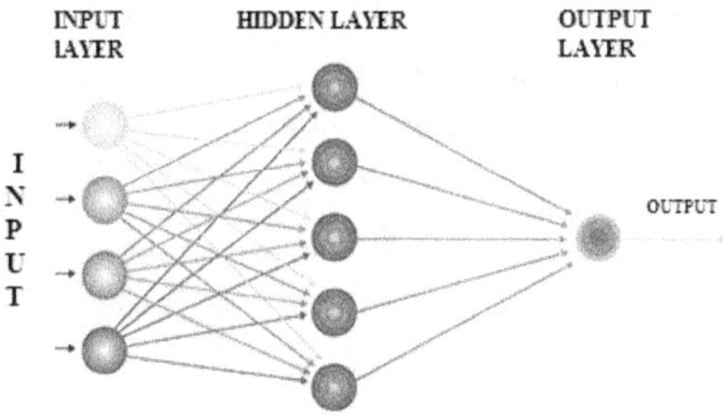

Figure 5.1: Artificial Neural Networks

The initial approach in this method is feature reduction. After giving input dataset, it undergoes several pre-processing based on that a result will be generated. The result is passed to the word net that avoids the words which are all not meaningful and those unwanted words. After that, the resultant data is processed on the fuzzy logic to get the categorical text clustering.

5.3. Computational Complexity

Generally, the text clustering mainly focused on reducing dimensionality, removing irrelevant data, increasing learning accuracy and improving result comprehensibility. The solution produced by the existing algorithms like STIRR, ROCK & k-modes are not effective on above mentioned problems. The high dimensional vector space in which each aspect corresponds to a unique keyword. Along with this, the problem of extracting representative sentences from text is also not effective. Traditional machine learning algorithms like decision trees or artificial neural networks are examples of embedded approaches. The wrapper methods use the predictive accuracy of a pre-determined learning algorithm to determine the goodness of the selected subsets, the accuracy of the learning algorithms is usually high. However, the generality of the selected features is limited and the computational complexity is large and the filter methods are independent of learning.

The computational complexity of wrapper methods is low, but the accuracy of the learning algorithms is not guaranteed. The hybrid methods are a combination of filter and wrapper methods by using a filter method to reduce search space that will be considered by the subsequent wrapper. They mainly focus on combining filter and wrapper methods to achieve the best possible performance with a particular learning algorithm with similar time complexity of the filter methods. The wrapper methods are computationally expensive and tend to over fit on small training sets. The filter methods, in addition to their generality, are usually a good choice when the number of features is very large. With respect to the filter feature selection methods, the application of cluster analysis has been demonstrated to be more effective than traditional feature selection algorithms.

Feature subset selection can be viewed as the process of identifying and removing as many irrelevant and redundant features as possible. This is because ① irrelevant features do not contribute to the predictive accuracy and ② redundant features do not redound to getting a better predictor for that they provide mostly information which is already present in other feature(s). Of the many feature subset selection algorithms, few algorithms effectively eliminate irrelevant features but fail to handle redundant features yet some others can eliminate the irrelevant while taking care of the redundant features. Traditionally, feature subset selection research has focused on searching for relevant features.

5.4.   Design of Attributes

The number of initial clusters must be specified as input to the algorithm. If this number is too high, then duplicate clusters (i.e. clusters with identical membership values across all objects) are found. While it might appear at first sight that duplicate clusters can simply be removed after the algorithm has converged and membership subsequently renormalized to sum to one, this is not possible because of the coupling between membership values and Page Rank values. That is, it cannot be assumed that the current Page Rank values are correct under a renormalization of membership values. The solution is to perform a check for duplicate clusters at the completion of each maximization step. If duplicate clusters are found, membership values are renormalized and the algorithm is allowed to proceed until a stage at which convergence has been achieved and no duplicate clusters exist.

5.4.1.   Threshold of Similarity Values

Depending on the domain, the graph representing the relation between objects may be heavily or sparsely connected. In the case of sentence clustering, it is found that many of the similarities S_{ij} between sentences are very small and are likely to be spurious, arising from incidental similarities between words in sentences which are in fact not semantically related. In practice, it is also found that the clustering performance of the algorithm can be improved by thresholding. These similarity values are such that all values below the threshold are converted to zero. All sentence clustering results reported in this research works are based on thresholding similarity values such that 50 percent of the values in the affinity matrix are zero.

5.4.2. *Hard Clustering*

Hard clustering methods are based on classical set theory and require that an object either does or does not belong to a cluster. Hard clustering means partitioning the data into a specified number of mutually exclusive subsets. The algorithm outputs cluster membership values k, i, which represent the degree of membership of object i to cluster k. If hard clustering is required, this can be trivially achieved by assigning a sentence to the cluster m for which membership is highest.

5.5. Solution Strategies

The aim of a text clustering scheme is to minimizing intra-cluster distances between text and maximizing inter-cluster distances (using an appropriate distance measure between documents). A distance measure (or, dually, similarity measure) thus lies at the heart of text clustering. The large variety of documents makes it almost impossible to create a general algorithm which can work best in case of all kinds of datasets. The major use of document clustering is to give users an overview of the contents of a document collection and reduce search space. If a collection is well clustered, search only the clusters that will contain relevant text. Efficiency and effectiveness can be improved by searching through smaller collection itself.

Text categorization is the task of assigning a Boolean value to each pair $\langle d_j, c_i \rangle \in D \times C$, where D is a set of documents and $C = \{c_1, \ldots, c_{|c|}\}$ is a set of predefined categories. A value of T assigned to $\langle d_j, c_i \rangle$ indicates a decision to file d_j under c_i, while a value of F indicates a decision not to file d_j under c_i. In general, the task is to approximate the unknown target function: $f' : D \times C \rightarrow \{\text{true, false}\}$ that describes how documents ought to be classified by means of a function $f : D \times C \rightarrow \{\text{true, false}\}$ called the classifier such that f' and f coincide as much as possible. Different constraints may be enforced on the Text Clustering (TC) task, depending on the application. TC may be either a single-labeled (i.e. exactly one $c_i \in C$ must be assigned to each $d_j \in D$) or a multi-labeled (i.e. any number $0 \le n_j \le |C|$ of categories may be assigned to a document $d_j \in D$). A special case of single-labeled TC is binary TC, in which, given category c_i, each $d_j \in D$ must be assigned either to $\overline{C_i}$ or to its complement c_i. A classifier for c_i is then a function $f'_i : D \rightarrow \{\text{true, false}\}$ that approximates the unknown target function $f_i : D \rightarrow \{\text{true, false}\}$. The problem of multi-label TC under $C = \{c_1, \ldots, c_{|c|}\}$ is usually tackled as $|C|$ independent binary classification problems under $\{\overline{C_i}, c_i\}$, for $i = 1, \ldots, |C|$. In this case, a classifier for C is thus actually composed of $|C|$ binary classifiers.

5.5.1. *Clustering Famous Quotation*

The algorithm is applied to clustering famous quotations and they provide a rich and challenging context for evaluating sentence clustering because they often contain a lot of semantic information (i.e. wisdom packed into a small message) and are often couched in a poetic use of language. An external clustering evaluation criterion has been applied (which requires that the true groupings is known) and then compiled a database of famous quotations from five different classes. The quotations are taken from an extract. Although there is some degree of word overlap between quotations, this is not sufficient to allow adequate measure of similarity by using a conventional bag of words approach.

The quality of data affects the data mining results. In order to improve the quality of data and consequently of the mining results, raw data is pre-processed so as to improve the efficiency and ease of mining process. In the proposed system, pre-processing for dataset is done to remove the stop words and stem words which are considered as less important and to improve quality and efficiency of data. Many of the most frequently used words in English are useless in Information Retrieval (IR) and text mining. Stop-words, which are language-specific functional words, are frequent words that carry no information (i.e. pronouns, prepositions, conjunctions). Examples of such words include 'the', 'of,' and', 'to', etc. These stop words are get stored in the database. Dataset (famous quotations) is loaded into another database. The stop words in data set (famous quotation) are removed by comparing with the stop word database. The number of initial clusters must be specified as input to the algorithm. If this number is too high, then duplicate clusters (i.e. clusters with identical membership values across all objects) are found.

Sentence clustering plays an important role in many text processing activities. For example, various authors have argued that incorporating sentence clustering into extractive multi-document summarization helps avoid problems of content overlap, leading to better coverage. However, sentence clustering is used within more general text mining tasks. For example, consider web mining, where the specific objective might be to discover relevant novel information from a set of documents initially retrieved in response to some query. By clustering the sentences of those documents it would intuitively expected that at least one of the clusters to be closely related to the concepts described by the query terms; however, other clusters may contain information pertaining to the query in some way hitherto unknown and in such a case it would have successfully mined new information.

The most quotations will contain interrelated topics or themes and many sentences will be related to some degree to a number of these. The work described in this research work is motivated by the belief that successfully being able to capture such fuzzy relationships will lead to an increase in the breadth and scope of problems to which sentence clustering can be applied. However, clustering text at the sentence level poses specific challenges not present when clustering larger segments of text such as documents.

The famous quotations data sets have been constructed in order to evaluate the performance of the algorithm by using standard external cluster quality criteria. To demonstrate how the algorithm may be of more general use in activities related to text mining, the algorithm has been applied to clustering sentences from a recent news article.

5.5.2. *Measuring Sentence Similarity*

Document comparison process generates frequent term sets for the given document with minimum support from 5 to 95 after subjected to the document pre-processing task (stopword removal and stemming process). Then, it is compared with the trained document available in the database one by one and finds out the matching percentage. Binary searching technique is used to search a term from the trained document database during matching process because of its competency/efficiency. The procedure accepts the document name to perform stopword removal, stemming and frequent term set generation pre-processing steps. Initially, a minimum support of 5% is considered to generate frequent term set. Then this frequent term sets are compared with every trained document in the database to determine the matching percentage after that the minimum support is increased by 5% and then performs the matching percentage once again with the entire trained document to evaluate the matching percentage. This process is repeated until the matching percentage is reached to 95% or maximum (all) document matching becomes 100%.

To calculate similarity values S_{ij} for the affinity matrix, a modified version of the measure has been proposed. This approach is similar to that used to calculate document similarity in the IR literature; however, rather than using a common vector space representation for all sentences, the two sentences being compared are represented in a reduced vector space of dimension n, where n is the number of distinct nonstop words appearing in the two sentences. Semantic vectors, V_1 and V_2, representing sentences S_1 and S_2 in the reduced vector space are first constructed. The elements of V_i are determined as follows: Let V_{ij} be the jth element of V_i and let w_j be the word corresponding to dimension j in the reduced vector space. Once V_1 and V_2 have been determined, the semantic similarity between S_1 and S_2 is defined by using a standard measure of similarity. The sentence similarity measure relies on a word-to-word semantic similarity measure. Many such measures have been proposed and can broadly be categorized as either corpus-based, in which case the similarity is calculated based on distributional information derived from large corpora and knowledge-based, in which similarity is based on semantic relations expressed in external resources such as dictionaries or thesauri.

$$sim(v_1, v_2) = \frac{1}{IC(v_1) + IC(v_2) - 2 * IC(LCS(v_1, v_2))}$$

Applying this distance formula to a word sense disambiguation task, an improvement where multiple sense words have been disambiguated by finding the combination of senses from a set of contiguous terms which minimizes total pair wise distance between senses. Hence, it is found that the performance is robust under a number of perturbations; however, depth factor scaling and restricting the type of link to a strictly hierarchical relation do noticeably impair performance.

Similarity calculation is mainly based on number of terms which is common between two sentences by number of words present in both sentences. Based on sentence similarity, sentences with highest Page Rank value are taken through Page Rank algorithm. Page Rank algorithm provides the importance of sentence i.e. how many times the sentence appears in the document and then fuzzy clustering algorithm is applied. Mixing coefficients are initialized such that priors for all clusters are equal. In expectation step, Page Rank value for each object in each cluster is calculated. Page Rank algorithm provides the importance of sentence i.e. how many times the sentence appears in the document. Maximization step involves only the single step of updating the mixing coefficients based on membership values calculated in the Expectation Step.

The ability to accurately judge the similarity between natural language sentences is critical to the performance of several applications such as text mining, question answering and text summarization. Given two sentences, an effective similarity measure should be able to determine whether the sentences are semantically equivalent or not, taking into account the variability of natural language expression. Similarity between two sentences is provided by Text rank measure. Assume that cluster membership values are initialized randomly and normalized such that cluster membership for an object sums to unity over all clusters. Mixing coefficients are initialized such that priors for all clusters are equal.

The dataset used for this research work is famous quotation dataset where a large number of documents are available for usage and they are analyzed offline. There are certain advantages in the work of semantic association discovery by combining a taxonomy structure with corpus statistics. The incorporation of a manually built pseudo knowledge base (e.g. thesaurus or taxonomy) may complement the statistical approach where "true" understanding of the text is unobtainable. By doing this, the statistics model can take advantage of a conceptual space structured by a hand-crafted taxonomy, while providing computational evidence from manoeuvring in the conceptual space via distributional analysis of data. In other words, calculating the semantic association can be transformed to the estimation of the conceptual similarity (or distance) between nodes (words or concepts) in the conceptual space generated by the taxonomy. Ideally, this kind of knowledge base should be reasonably broad-coverage, well-structured and easily manipulated in order to derive desired associative or similarity information.

5.6. Recent Trends in Fuzzy

Applications of Fuzzy Logic in Data Mining: This section focuses on real-world applications of fuzzy techniques for data mining. It first gives a brief presentation of the theoretical background common to all applications, decomposed into two main elements: the notion of similarity and the fuzzy machine learning techniques that are applied in the described applications. Indeed, similarity, or more generally comparison measures are used at all levels of the data mining and information retrieval tasks: at the lowest level, they are used for the matching between a query to a database and the elements it contains, for the extraction of relevant data. Then similarity and dissimilarity measures can be used in the process of cleaning and management of missing data to create a training set. In the various techniques to generalize particular information contained in this training set, dissimilarity measures are used in the case of inductive learning, similarity measures for case-based reasoning or clustering tasks.

Eventually, similarities are used to interpret results of the learning process into an expressible form of knowledge, for instance through the definition of prototypes. Real-World Fuzzy Logic Applications Characterization of data sets and fuzzy clustering that identifies relevant subgroups in data sets. Finally describes real world applications exploiting these methods and belonging both to the data mining and information retrieval fields. They cover several domains, such as medical, educational, chemical and multimedia.

Real World Applications

In this section, a panel of real-world fuzzy logic applications is presented, based on the similarity framework and the fuzzy learning methods described in the previous section. They belong both to the data mining and information retrieval fields, and cover several domains, namely medical, educational, and multimedia. For each application, the objective of the task, the considered data, the applied method and the obtained results are successively described.

Medical Applications

Medical applications are good cases where Fuzzy Set Theory can bring out enhancement as compared to classic algorithms because most of the attributes used here to characterize cases are associated with imprecise values. In this section, presents three applications of data mining, respectively to prevent cardio-vascular diseases, to measure asthma severity and to detect malign micro calcifications in mammographies. Data Mining to Prevent Cardio-Vascular Diseases: This project was done thanks to financial supports by INSERM and was led by M.-C. Jaulent (INSERM ERM 0202). Researchers from several French universities collaborated with a medical scientist on a well-known database to prevent cardio-vascular diseases. Objective: The main objective here was to find discriminating features in order to prevent cardio-vascular diseases. Predictions should help medical scientists to detect and prevent cardio-vascular diseases for hypertensive patients.

Educational Applications

Providing Interpretable Characterizations of Students: In this section, consider another domain application for fuzzy machine learning methods, namely the educational domain. The presented application was performed in the framework of a project with the schoolbook publisher Bordas-Nathan. Objective: The considered task consists in characterizing students, through the identification of relevant groups of students having the same characteristics, and the comparison of several student classes, to determine whether the classes present the same characteristics or not. Of special importance is the interpretability of the results, to enable a teacher to exploit the information and the structure identified in the student data.

Multimedia Applications

In this section, consider applications in data mining and information retrieval in the multimedia field. It describes first an image retrieval application based on a visual similarity navigation paradigm and seconds a learning approach for a semantic annotation of a video signal, based on some examples. Searching in a Clothes Catalogue by Visual Similarity: This work is part of the results of the ITEA European project: KLIMT-KnowLedge InterMedation Technology. Although in this project several laboratories and industry partners were involved to accomplish what follows, the company Sinequa played a significant role. Objective: The main objective of this work was to enhance a classic text search engine of an on-line clothes catalogue, with an image search tool. A prototype has been developed that illustrated the complementarities between the two navigation schemas: text queries and visual-similarity browsing.

Fuzzy Logic in Various Fields

In "Comparison of Detection and Classification Algorithms using Boolean and Fuzzy Techniques" by Rahul Dixit and Harpreet Singh, the authors compare various logic analysis methods and present results for a hypothetical target classification scenario. They show how preprocessing can reasonably preserve result confidence and compare the results between Boolean, multi-quantization Boolean, and fuzzy techniques.

In "A Fuzzy Pre-Processing Module for Optimizing the Access Network Selection in Wireless Networks" by Faisal Kaleem, Abolfazl Mehbodniya, Kang K. Yen, and Fumiyuki Adachi, the authors present the design and implementation of a fuzzy multi-criteria scheme for vertical handoff necessity estimation. Their method determines the proper time for vertical handoff while considering the continuity and quality of the currently utilized service and end-user satisfaction.

In "A Soft Computing Approach to Crack Detection, Impact Source Identification with Field-Programmable Gate Array Implementation" by Arati M. Dixit and Harpreet Singh, the authors present a fuzzy inference system to automate crack detection and impact source identification (CDISI) and present their work on a microchip for automated CDISI.

In "Analysis of Adaptive Fuzzy Technique for Multiple Crack Diagnosis of Faulty Beam Using Vibration Signatures" by Amiya Kumar Dash, the author proposes a method for multi-crack detection of structure using a fuzzy Gaussian technique.

In "Effect of Road Traffic Noise Pollution on Human Work Efficiency in Government Offices, Private Organizations, and Commercial Business Centres in Agartala City Using Fuzzy Expert System-A Case Study" by Debasish Pal and Debasish Bhattacharya, the authors examine the reduction in human work efficiency due to growing road traffic noise pollution. Using fuzzy logic, they monitor and model disturbances from vehicular road traffic and the effect on personal work performance.

In "A Hybrid Approach to Failure Analysis using Stochastic Petri Nets and Ranking Generalized Fuzzy Numbers" by Abolfazl Doostparast Torshizi and Jamshid Parvizian, the authors present an innovative failure analysis approach that combines the flexibility of fuzzy logic with the structural properties of stochastic Petri Nets. This algorithm has a diverse range of industrial applications.

In "Excluded-Mean-Variance Neural Decision Processor for Qualitative Group Decision Making" by Ki-Young Song, Janusz Kozinski, Gerald T.G. Seniuk, and Madan M. Gupta, the authors introduce an innovative mean-variance neural approach for group decision making in uncertain situations. The authors provide a case study with the excluded-mean-variance approach that shows this approach can improve the effectiveness of qualitative decision making by providing the decision maker with a new cognitive tool to assist in the reasoning process.

In "Warren, McCain, and Obama Needed Fuzzy Sets at Presidential Forum" by Ashu M. G. Solo, the author shows how the moderator and presidential candidates in a presidential forum needed fuzzy logic to properly ask and answer a debate question. The author shows how an understanding of fuzzy logic is needed to properly ask and answer queries about defining imprecise linguistic terms. Then Solo distinguishes between qualitative definitions and quantitative definitions of imprecise linguistic terms and distinguishes between crisp quantitative definitions and fuzzy quantitative definitions of imprecise linguistic terms.

In "A Fuzzy Rule-Based Expert System for Evaluating Intellectual Capital" by Mohammad Hossein Fazel Zarandia, Neda Mohammadhasanb, and Susan Bastanic, the authors describe their fuzzy expert system for evaluating intellectual capital. This assists managers in understanding and evaluating the level of each asset created through intellectual activities.

5.7.   Fuzzy Based Architectural Design

Based on the above observation, Fuzzy based algorithm has been proposed in which the result belongs to a single cluster. A semantic clustering and fuzzy based pruning approach is practiced to bring more accuracy in mining process. Generally, fuzzy clustering based on the prototypes or mixtures of Gaussians which does not support sentence clustering. The algorithm indentifies the semantically related sentences and avoids duplication on the given data set. The information retrieval based on the keyword in which filtering is processed on the benchmark dataset. Fuzzy sets are closely related to the definition of similarities because of their capacity to represent subjective information, resulting from real world complexity and gray areas of interpretation and because of the graduality inherent in their definition, in agreement with the natural behavior of intuitive similarities. An overview of similarities has been proposed in the framework of fuzzy logic, similarity measures enabling the user to preserve the flexibility and graduality human beings have in mind when they deal with similarities and use expressions such as "very similar", "rather similar", "more similar than", etc.,

Fuzzy clustering is important in domains such as sentence clustering, since a sentence is related to more than one theme or topic present within a document or set of documents. In the proposed system, Fuzzy clustering algorithm operates on Expectation-Maximization framework in which the cluster membership probabilities for sentence in each cluster are identified. Results obtained while applying the algorithm to sentence clustering tasks demonstrate that the algorithm is capable of identifying overlapping clusters of semantically related sentences and its performance improvement can be proved by comparing with k-medoid. Performance measures such as Purity, Entropy, Partition-Entropy and V-Measure are used to prove the performance improvement of document clustering and its application in document summarization.

The research work demonstrates to stress on the fact that many of the measures, methods and properties which are pointed out can be used in a general environment, not necessarily involving a fuzzy set based representation, the fuzziness and graduality appearing in the only similarities themselves. There exist various types of similarity measures: for binary data, for fuzzy data, for numerical data, for structured data, etc., This work focuses on classical definitions related to binary data and their extensions to fuzzy data in a general formalization incorporating most of the well known measures, classifying them and proposing new ones, to help the user to choose one of them according to the problem.

Fuzzy uses weighting schemes for the process of information retrieval in which it also assess the importance of whole attributes and individual values in the dataset. The work is intended immediate retrieval of response based on the input query. Based on the query, the clusters are done which related to the concepts based on the given queries by the user. The page rank algorithm has been used which was developed by Diane Kelly [2009].

$$xy(v_i) = (1-d) * \sum_{j \in n(v_i)} \frac{1}{|out(v_j)|} xy(v_j)$$

where v_i points in and v_j points out on the set of vertices. The similarity between the v_j and v_i based on the similarity as store these are stored on the matrix form such as $W = (w_{ij})$ that refers to the affinity matrix. This can expressed on the below equations and the following steps.

$$xy(v_i) = (1-d) + d * \sum_{j=1}^{N} (w_{ij} \frac{xy(v_j)}{\sum_{k=1}^{N} w_{jk}})$$

1. Compute the similarity between all pairs of clusters i.e. calculates a similarity matrix whose ij^{th} entry gives the similarity between the ith and j^{th} clusters.
2. Merge the most similar (closest) two clusters.
3. Update the similarity matrix to reflect the pairwise similarity between the new cluster and the original clusters.
4. Repeat steps 2 and 3 until only a single cluster remains.

The overall Fuzzy based categorical text clustering steps is given in Figure 5.2.

<table>
<tr><td>

1. Fragment each sentence into single words and those words are passed into the word net
2. Filter conjunctions and keywords
3. Retrieval decision is made by comparing the terms of query with index terms
4. Validate the duplication in the word net and determine the frequency of occurrence
5. Form semantic clustering based on Fuzzy based pruning approach
    a. The similarity matrix can be formed using sim = {simxy} where x and y is the similarity between the objects.
6. The weight between the matrices is W_{ij}^{c} where c is the cluster
7. Similarity matrix is calculated using
    Sim$_{x\&y}$ (w1, w2) = 1/(IC (w1) + IC (w2) – 2 * IC (DCS (w1, w2))) where w are the words from the information content, IC are the information content and DCS is deepest common similarity.
8. IC (w) is calculated by IC (w) = -log P (w) that is probability of the word w appear in the IC information content.

</td></tr>
</table>

Figure 5.2: Fuzzy based Categorical Text Clustering Algorithm

The results of the experiment confirm that the information content approach proposed provides a significant improvement over the traditional edge counting method. It also shows that the proposed combined fuzzy approach outperforms the information content approach. One should recognize that even a small percentage improvement over the existing approaches is of significance since the results are nearing the observed upper bound.

5.8. Architectural Design

As a document set may contain several thousands of words, it results in a very high impracticable dimensionality. To reduce the document space dimensionality, word reduction methods are applied in the pre-processing phase. The most common method to reduce the number of different words is to eliminate the words with low information value. The stemming algorithm is used in text clustering to remove suffixes from the words in order to determine the common root of the words.

Another way to reduce the document space dimensionality is based on the statistical properties of the word. The infrequent and frequent words are filtered out from the original text. The reduction is based on the assumption that, in the words with low frequency, is not a characteristic word for the document set. The weight of a word is measured by its frequency count with respect to minimum support threshold value.

The steps involved in the architecture shown in Figure 5.3 are discussed below:

Collection of Data: The famous quotations data set was constructed in order to evaluate performance of the algorithm using standard external cluster quality criteria. To demonstrate how the algorithm may be of more general use in activities related to text mining, the algorithm has been applied to clustering sentences from a recent news article includes the processes like crawling, indexing, filtering etc., which are used to collect the documents that need to be clustered, index them to store and retrieve in a better way and filter them to remove the extra data, for example, stop words. The number of documents on the internet is continuously increasing due to large amount of online sources available and it is very difficult for the users to go through all the sources and find the relevant information from the collection.

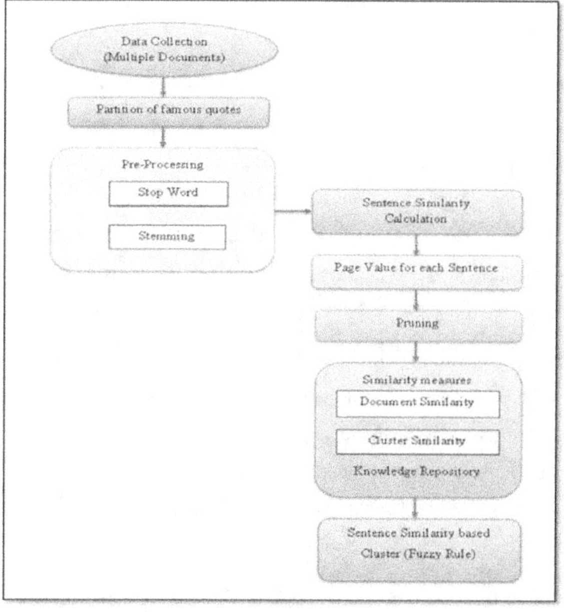

Figure 5.3: Architecture of Fuzzy based Categorical Text Clustering System

The sentences of those documents, at least one of the clusters to be closely related to the concepts described by the query terms; however, other clusters may contain information pertaining to the query in some way hitherto unknown to us and in such a case new information is mined successfully. Irrespective of the specific task (e.g. summarization, text mining, etc.), most documents will contain interrelated topics or themes and many sentences will be related to some degree to a number of these. This work concentrates in determining the global importance of a sentence; i.e. how important a sentence is in the context of the paper as a whole, irrespective of its membership to individual clusters.

Pre-processing: Raw data is highly concerned with noise, missing values and inconsistency and the quality of data affects the data mining results. In order to improve the quality of data and consequently of the mining results, raw data is pre-processed so as to improve the efficiency and ease of mining process. In the proposed system, pre-processing for dataset is done to remove the stop words and stem words which are considered as less important and to improve quality and efficiency of data. Many of the most frequently used words in English are useless in Information Retrieval and text mining. These words are called 'Stopwords'. It consists of steps that take as input a plain text document and output a set of tokens (which can be single terms or n-grams) to be included in the vector model. Filtering is the process of removing special characters and punctuation that are not thought to hold any discriminative power under the vector model. This is more critical in the case of formatted documents, such as web pages where formatting tags can either be discarded or identified and their constituent terms attributed different weights. Term Frequency Weighting methods are applicable only when the selected terms of the documents are known in advance. In new document environment, frequent term set generation is the most applicable method to find frequent terms as well as for dimension reduction. Frequent terms are determined by scanning the document and collecting those terms that satisfy the minimum support threshold value.

Tokenization: Tokenization splits sentences into individual tokens, typically words. More sophisticated methods, drawn from the field of NLP, parse the grammatical structure of the text to pick significant terms or chunks, such as noun phrases. Stemming is the process of reducing words to their base form or stem. For example, the words "connected", "connection", "connections" are all reduced to the stem "connect". Porter's algorithm is the de facto standard stemming algorithm.

Stop word removal: A stop word is defined as a term, which is not thought to convey any meaning as a dimension in the vector space (i.e. without context). A typical method to remove stop words is to compare each term with a compilation of known stop words. Another approach is to first apply a parts-of-speech tagger and then reject all tokens that are not nouns, verbs and adjectives.

In computer search engines, a stop word is a commonly used word (such as "the") that a search engine has been programmed to ignore, both when indexing entries for searching and when retrieving them as the result of a search query. When building the index, most engines are programmed to remove certain words from any index entry. The list of words that are not to be added is called a stop list. Stop words are deemed irrelevant for searching purposes because they occur frequently in the language for which the indexing engine has been tuned. In order to save both space and time, these words are dropped at indexing time and then ignored at search time. Some search engines allow one to include a stop word in a search by putting an inclusion (plus sign) before each stop word in the query. Sometimes, some extremely common words which would appear to be of little value in helping select documents matching a user need are excluded from the vocabulary entirely (stopwords). The general strategy for determining a stop list is to sort the terms by collection frequency (the total number of times each term appears in the document collection) and then to take the most frequent terms, often hand-filtered for their semantic content relative to the domain of the documents being indexed, as a stop list, the members of which are then discarded during indexing. Stop words are removed from the index and the query. Words might carry little meaning from a frequency (or information theoretic) point of view and alternatively from a linguistic point of view. Words that occur in many of the documents in the collection carry little meaning from a frequency point of view.

Stemming: One challenge emerging, when terms are defined as single words, is that the feature space becomes very highly dimensional. In addition, words which are in the same context, such as biology and biologist are defined as different terms. So, in order to define words that are in the same context with the same term and consequently to reduce dimensionality, the terms are defined as stemmed words. A stemmer applies morphological 'rules of the thumb' to normalize words. Stemming tends to help as many queries as it hurts. Sometimes stemming algorithms may conflate two words with very different meanings to the same stem, for instance the words "skies" and "ski" will both be reduced to "ski". In such cases users might not understand why a certain document is retrieved and may begin to question the integrity of the system in general. Still, stemmers are used often in many research systems like Smart, Okapi and Twenty-One. The In Query System uses a stemming technique called K-stem that combines dictionary lookup and stemming rules.

In most cases, morphological variants of words have similar semantic interpretations and are considered as equivalent for the purpose of IR applications. For this reason, a number of so-called stemming algorithms and stemmers, have been developed, which attempt to reduce a word to its stem or root form. Thus, the key terms of a query or document are represented by stems rather than by the original words. This not only means that different variants of a term can be conflated to a single representative form and it also reduces the dictionary size, that is, the number of distinct terms needed for representing a set of documents. A smaller dictionary size results in a saving of storage space and processing time.

Keyword stemming: Keyword stemming is a useful tool for web pages and search engine optimization. The process of keyword stemming involves taking a basic but popular keyword pertaining to a particular website and adding a prefix, suffix and pluralization to make the keyword into a new word. This particular process allows a website to expand upon the number of variable options, which can help a website get more traffic. Words that are a product of keyword stemming can expand in either direction and even add words to the phrase, making the possibilities limitless.

Sentence Similarity calculation: The ability to accurately judge the similarity between natural language sentences is critical to the performance of several applications such as text mining, question answering and text summarization. Given two sentences, an effective similarity measure should be able to determine whether the sentences are semantically equivalent or not, taking into account the variability of natural language expression. Similarity between two sentences is provided by Text Rank measure. A different approach proposes to extract the dissimilarity relation directly from the data by guiding the extraction process itself with as little supervision as possible.

$$Similarity\ (S_i,\ S_j) = \{\ W_k\ |\ W_k \in S_i,\ W_k \in S_j\}/log(|S_i|) + log\ (|S_j|)$$

Where W_k denotes number of terms common between two sentences *(Si, Sj)*

$log(|S_i|)$ denotes number of words in sentence *i* and

$log\ (|S_j|$ denotes number of words in sentence *j*

Page Value: By means of Page Rank algorithm, Page Rank value for each sentence is calculated. Calculating the importance of a sentence is that sentences which are similar to a large number of other important sentences are central. Thus, by ranking sentences according to their centrality, the top ranking sentences can then be extracted and provided as input to our proposed algorithm.

Pruning: Pruning removes words that appear with very low frequency throughout the corpus. The underlying assumption is that these words, even if they had any discriminating power, would form too small clusters to be useful. A pre-specified threshold is typically used, e.g. a small fraction of the number of words in the corpus. Sometimes words which occur too frequently (e.g. in 40% or more of the documents) are also removed.

Post processing: Post processing includes the major applications, in which the document clustering is used, e.g. the application that uses the results of clustering for recommending news articles to the users.

Summary

The problem of text clustering is generally defined as follows: given a set of document clustering. An automatically derived number of clusters, such that the documents assigned to each cluster are more similar to each other than the documents assigned to different clusters. Texts are represented by using the vector space model that treats a document as a bag of words. A major characteristic of document clustering algorithms is the high dimensionality of the feature space, which imposes a big challenge to the performance of clustering algorithms. They could not work efficiently in high dimensional feature spaces due to the inherent sparseness of the data. The next challenge is that not all features are important for document clustering, some of the features may be redundant or irrelevant and some may even misguide the clustering result, especially there are more irrelevant more features than relevant ones.

The wrapper methods use the predictive accuracy of a predetermined learning algorithm to determine the goodness of the selected subsets, the accuracy of the learning algorithms is usually high. However, the generality of the selected features is limited and the computational complexity is large and the filter methods are independent of learning. Fuzzy based algorithm has been proposed in which the result belongs to a single cluster and a semantic clustering and Fuzzy based pruning approach is practiced to bring more accuracy in mining process. Fuzzy uses weighting schemes for the process of information retrieval in which it also assess the importance of whole attributes and individual values in the dataset. The works is intended immediate retrieval of response based on the input query. Based on the query, the clusters are done which are related to the concepts based on the given queries by the user.

The famous quotations data set was constructed in order to evaluate performance of the algorithm by using standard external cluster quality criteria. The overall algorithm is presented to prove the concepts used. To demonstrate how the algorithm may be of more general use in activities related to text mining, the algorithm has been applied to clustering sentences from a recent news article.

1. Give a short note on fuzzy categorical clustering.

2. Briefly discuss about the artificial neural network.

3. Discuss in short about the applications of fuzzy logic in data mining.

4. Write in brief about fuzzy logic applications in real world.

5. Write a short note on recent trends in fuzzy logic.

BIBLIOGRAPHY

[1]. J. Abonyi, M.D. Alexiuk, P. Angelov and B. Bird, "Advances in Fuzzy Clustering and its applications", John Wiley & Sons, Ltd, 2007.

[2]. A. Abraham, "It is time to Fuzzify Neural Networks", Proceedings International Conference on Intelligent Multimedia and Distance Education, Pp. 253-273, 2001.

[3]. R. Agrawal, J. Gehrke, D. Gunopulos and P. Raghavan, "Automatic subspace clustering of high dimensional data for data mining applications", SIGMOD'98, 1998.

[4]. A. Nishant, A. Gautam and N. Sharma, "Use of Logic Gates to Make Edge Avoider Robot", International Journal of Information & Computation Technology, Vol.4, No.6, 2014.

[5]. S. Albayrak and F. Armasyali, "Fuzzy C-Means Clustering on Medical Diagnostic System", Proceeding of the XIIth Turkish Symposium on Artificial Intelligent Network, 2003.

[6]. K. Alsabti, S. Ranka and V. Singh, "CLOUDS: A Decision Tree Classifier for Large Datasets", Conference on Knowledge Discovery and Data Mining, 1998.

[7]. M.R. Anderberg, "Cluster Analysis for Applications", Academic Press, Inc., New York, 1973.

[8]. Andrew Skabar and Khaled Abdalgader, "Clustering Sentence-Level Text Using a Novel Fuzzy Relational Clustering Algorithm", IEEE Transactions on Knowledge and Data Engineering, Vol. 25, No. 1, 2013.

[9]. P. Andritsos, P. Tsaparas., R. Miller and K. Sevcik, "LIMBO: Scalable Clustering of Categorical Data", EDBT Conference, 2004.

[10]. A.K. Jain and R.C. Dubes, "Algorithms for Clustering Data, Prentice Hall", Englewood Clis, New Jersey, 1988.

[11]. M. Ankerst, M. Breunig., H.P. Kriegel and J. Sander, "Optics: Ordering points to identify the clustering structure", SIGMOD, 1999.

[12]. R.A. Baeza-Yates and B.A. Ribeiro-Neto., "Modern Information Retrieval - the concepts and technology behind search", Second edition, Pearson Education Ltd., Harlow, England, 2011.

[13]. L. Baker and A. McCallum, "Distributional Clustering of Words for Text Classification", ACM SIGIR Conference, 1998.

[14]. G.H. Ball and D.J. Hall, "A clustering technique for summarizing multivariate data", Behavioral Science, Vol. 12, Pp.153–155, 1967.

[15]. R. Bekkerman, R. El-Yaniv, Y. Winter and N. Tishby, "On Feature Distributional Clustering for Text Categorization", ACM SIGIR Conference, 2001.

[16]. S. Belhassen and H. Zaidi, "A Novel Fuzzy C-Means Algorithm for Unsupervised Heterogeneous Tumor Quantification in PET", Medical Physics, Vol.37, No.3, Pp.1309–1324, 2010.

[17]. Bernadette Plug-sucker, "The Fuzzy Logic", University Press of France, 1993.

[18]. J.C. Bezdek, "Pattern Recognition with Fuzzy Objective Function", Plenum Press, 1981.

[19]. J.C. Bezdek, "Pattern Recognition with Fuzzy Objective Function Algorithms", Kluwer Academic Publishers, Norwell, MA, USA, 1981.

[20]. L. Bobrowski and J.C. Bezdek, "c-Means clustering with the L1 and L1 norms", IEEE Transactions on Systems, Man and Cybernetics, Vol.21, No.3, Pp.545–554, 1991.

[21]. M. Blej and M. Azizi, "Task Parameters Managing and System Accuracy in Fuzzy Real Time Scheduling", International Journal of Engineering Sciences & Research Technology, 2016.

[22]. J. Catlett, "Mega induction: Machine Learning on Vary Large Databases", Ph.D, University of Sydney, 1991.

[23]. P.K. Chan and S.J. Stolfo, "On the Accuracy of Meta-learning for Scalable Data Mining", Journal of Intelligent Information Systems, Vol.8, Pp.5-28, 1997.

[24]. C. Ballard, D. Herreman, D. Schau, R. Bell, E. Kim and A. Valencic, "Data modeling techniques for data warehousing", IBM Corporation International Technical Support Organization, 1998.

[25]. D. Cutting, D. Karger, J. Pedersen and J. Tukey, "Scatter/Gather: A Cluster-based Approach to Browsing Large Document Collections", ACM SIGIR Conference, 1992.

[26]. M. Dash, S.T. Tan and H. Liu, "Entropy-Based Fuzzy Clustering and Fuzzy Modeling", Fuzzy Sets and System, Vol.113, Pp.381–388, 2000.

[27]. David Gibson, Jon M. Kleinberg and Prabhakar Raghavan , "Clustering Categorical Data: An Approach Based on Dynamical Systems", Proceedings of the 24th International Conference on Very Large Data Bases (VLDB), Pp.311-322, 1998.

[28]. M. Dembo and Y.l. Wang, "Stresses at the cell-to-substrate interface during locomotion of fibroblasts", Biophys Journal, Vol.76, Pp.2307–2316, 1999.

[29]. M. Sabeghi and H. Deldari, "Fuzzy Algorithm for Scheduling Periodic Tasks on Multiprocessor", IJCSN International Journal of Computer Science and Network Security, Vol.6, No.3, 2006.

[30]. E. Diday and J.C. Simon, "Clustering Analysis In Digital Pattern Recognition", Education Springer, New Jercy, Pp.47–94, 1976.

[31]. Didier Dubois and Henri Prade, "The three semantics of fuzzysets", Fuzzy Sets and Systems, Pp.141-150, 1997.

[32]. Didier Dubois and Henri Prade, "Encyclopedia of Computer Science", 4th edition, Pp.734-742, 2003.

[33]. R. Dubes and A.K. Jian, "Validity studies in clustering methodologies", Pattern Recognition, Vol.11, Pp.235–254, 1979.

[34]. J.C. Dunn, "A Fuzzy Relative of the ISODATA Process and Its Use in Detecting Compact Well-Separated Clusters", Journal Cybernet, Vol. 3, Pp.32–57, 1973.

[35]. M. Ester, H.P. Kriegel, J. Sander and X. Xu, "A density-based algorithm for discovering clusters in large spatial databases", KDD, 1996.

[36]. D.J. Fifield, "Distributed Tree Construction from Large Datasets", Bachelor's Honor Thesis, Australian National University, 1992.

[37]. X. Freitas and S.H. Lavington, "Mining Very Large Databases with Parallel Processing", Kluwer Academic Publishers, 1998.

[38]. L. Fu and E. Medico, "FLAME: A Novel Fuzzy Clustering Method for the Analysis of DNA Microarray Data", BMC Bioinformatics, Vol.8, No.3, Pp.1-15, 2007.

[39]. J. Gehrke, R. Ramakrishnan and V. Ganti, "RainForest - A Framework for Fast Decision Tree Construction of Large Datasets", Data Mining and Knowledge Discovery, Vol.4, No.2/3, Pp.127-162, 2000.

[40]. T.Geweniger, D.Zuhlke, B.Hammer and T. Villmann, "Median Fuzzy C-Means for Clustering Dissimilarity Data", Neuro Computing, Vol.73, No.7-9, Pp.1109-1116, 2010.

[41]. J.M.Górriz, J.Ramírez, S.C.Alvarez, C.G.Puntonet, E.W. Lang and D.Erdogmus, "A Novel LMS Algorithm Applied to Adaptive Noise Cancellation", IEEE Signal Processing Letters, Vol.16, No.1, Pp.34 -37, 2009.

[42]. S. Guha, R. Rastogi and K. Shim, "An efficient clustering algorithm for large databases", SIGMOD, 1998.

[43]. S. Guha, R. Rastogi and K. Shim, "ROCK: a robust clustering algorithm for categorical attributes", International Conference on Data Engineering, 1999.

[44]. RJ. Hathaway and J.C. Bezdek, "Switching regression models and fuzzy clustering", IEEE Transactions on fuzzy systems, Vol.1, No.3, Pp.195–204, 1993.

[45]. Z. Huang, "Clustering large data sets with mixed numeric and categorical values", Proceedings of the First Pacific Asia Knowledge Discovery and Data Mining Conference, Pp.21–34, 1997.

[46]. Z. Huang, "A fast clustering algorithm to cluster very large categorical data sets in data mining", Proceedings of the SIGMOD Workshop on Research Issues on Data Mining and Knowledge Discovery, Canada, Pp.1–8, 1997.

[47]. Z. Huang and M.K. Ng., "A fuzzy K-modes algorithm for clustering categorical data", IEEE Transaction on Fuzzy Systems, Vol.7, No.4, Pp.446-452, 1999.

[48]. Z. Huang, "Extensions to the k-means algorithm for clustering large data sets with categorical values", Data Mining Knowledge Discover, Vol.2, No. 2, Pp.283-304, 1998.

[49]. N. Haman and D. Geogranas, "Comparison of Mamdani and Sugeno Fuzzy Inference Systems for Evaluating the Quality of Experience of Hapto-Audio-Visual Applications", IEEE International Workshop on Haptic Audio Visual Environments and their Applications, 2008.

[50]. S.M. Jagatheesan and V. Thiagarasu, "Design of a FUZZY logic based Categorical Text Clustering Algorithm for Information Retrieval", International Journal of Advanced Research in Computer Science and Software Engineering, Vol.4, No.1, Pp.981-984, 2014.

[51]. S.M. Jagatheesan and V. Thiagarasu, "Development of Fuzzy based categorical Text Clustering Algorithm for Information Retrieval", International Journal of Innovative Research in Computer and Communication Engineering, Vol.2, No.1, Pp.2740-2746, 2014.

[52]. A.K. Jain and R.C.Dubes, "Algorithms for Clustering Data. Prentice-Hall advanced reference series", Prentice-Hall, Inc., Upper Saddle River, New Jersey, 1988.

[53]. C.Z. Janikow, "Fuzzy Decision Trees: Issues and Methods", IEEE Transactions on Systems, Man, and Cybernetics, Vol.28, No.1, Pp.1-14, 1998.

[54]. Jeff Vitter, "Random sampling with a reservoir", ACM Transactions on Mathematical Software, Vol.11, No.1, Pp.37–57, 1985.

[55]. R. Jensi and G.WiselinJiji, "A Survey on Optimization Approaches To Text Document Clustering", International Journal on Computational Sciences & Applications (IJCSA), Vol.3, No.6, Pp.31-44, 2013.

[56]. L. Kaufman and P.J. Rousseeuw, "Finding groups in data", Wiley, New-York, 1990.

[57]. KiriWagsta, Claire Cardie, Seth Rogers and Stefan Schroedl, "Constrained K-means Clustering with Background Knowledge" Proceedings of the Eighteenth International Conference on Machine Learning, Pp.577-584, 2001.

[58]. S. Krinidis and V. Chatzis, "A Robust Fuzzy Local Information C-Means Clustering Algorithm", IEEE Transaction on Image Processing, Vol.19, No.5, Pp.1328–1337, 2010.

[59]. LiorRokach and OdedMaimon, "Decision Trees", Data mining and Knowledge Discovery Handbook, Pp.165-191

[60]. P. Ma and K. Chan, "Incremental Fuzzy Mining of Gene Expression Data for Gene Function Prediction", IEEE Transaction on Biomedical Engineering, 2010.

[61]. J. MacQueen, "Some methods for classification and analysis of multi variant observations", Proceeding of the Fifth Berkeley Symposium on Mathematics, Statistics and Probability, Vol.1, Pp.281-296, 1967.

[62]. Manpreetkaur and Usvir Kaur, "Comparison Between K-Mean and Hierarchical Algorithm Using Query Redirection", International Journal of Advanced Research in Computer Science and Software Engineering, Vol.3, No.7, Pp.1454-1459, 2013.

[63]. A. McCallum and K. Nigam, "A Comparison of Event Models for Naïve Bayes Text Classification", AAAI Workshop on Learning for Text Categorization, 1998.

[64]. W. McCulloch and Pitts W., "A Logical Calculus of the Ideas Immanent in Nervous Activity", Bulletin of Mathematical Biophysics, Vol.5, Pp.115-133, 1943.

[65]. M. Mehta, R.Agrawal and J.Rissanen, "SLIQ: A fast scalable classifier for Data Mining", Proceeding of the fifth International Conference on Extending Database Technology (EDBT), 1996.

[66]. R. Mihalcea and P. Tarau, "TextRank: Bringing Order into Texts", Proceedings of Conference on Empirical Methods in Natural Language (EMNLP), Pp. 404-411, 2004.

[67]. Mika Sato-Ilic and Lakhmi C. Jain, "Innovations in Fuzzy Clustering-Theory and Applications, Studies in Fuzziness and Soft Computing", Springer, Vol.205, 2006.

[68]. G.W. Milligan and M.C. Cooper, "An examination of procedures for determining the number of clusters in a data set", Psycho Metrika, Vol.50, No.2, Pp.159–179, 1985.

[69]. E.H. Mamdani and S. Assilian, "An experiment in linguistic synthesis with a fuzzy logic controller", International journal of man-machine studies, Vol.7, No.1, Pp.1-13, 1975.

[70]. R. Ng and J. Han, "Efficient and Effective Clustering Methods for Spatial Data Mining", VLDB Conference, 1994.

[71]. K. Nigam, A. McCallum, S. Thrun and T. Mitchell, "Learning to classify text from labelled and unlabeled documents", AAAI Conference, 1998.

[72]. V. Novák, I. Perfilieva and J. Močkoř, "Mathematical principles of fuzzy logic", Dodrecht: Kluwer Academic, 1999.

[73]. C. Olaru and L. Wehenkel, "A complete fuzzy decision tree technique", Fuzzy Sets and Systems, Vol.138, No.2, Pp.221–254, 2003.

[74]. N.R. Pal and J.C. Bezdek, "On Cluster Validity for the Fuzzy C-Means Model", IEEE FS, Vol.3, No.3, 1995.

[75]. Y. Peng, "Intelligent condition monitoring using fuzzy inductive learning", Journal of Intelligent Manufacturing, Vol.15, No.3, Pp.373-380, 2004.

[76]. D.K. Pratihar, "Soft Computing", Narosa Publishing House, New Delhi, India, 2008.

[77]. Qinbao Song, Jingjie Ni and Guangtao Wang, "A Fast Clustering-Based Feature Subset Selection Algorithm for High-Dimensional Data", IEEE Transactions on Knowledge and Data Engineering, Vol.25, No.1, 2013.

[78]. H. Ralambondrainy, "A conceptual version of the K-means algorithm", Pattern Recognition Letters, Vol.15, No. 11, Pp.1147-157, 1995.

[79]. L. Rokach and O. Maimon, "Data mining with decision trees: theory and applications", World Scientific Publication Co. Inc, 2008.

[80]. K. Ross and D. Srivastava, "Fast computation of sparse data cubes", In Proc. 1997 Int. Conf. Very Large Data Bases (VLDB'97), Pp.116–125, 1997.

[81]. Rudin Cynthia, "Sequential Event Prediction with Association Rules", 24th Annual Conference on Learning Theory (COLT), Pp.9-11, 2011.

[82]. E.R. Ruspini "A new approach to clustering", Information Control, Vol.19, Pp.22–32, 1969.

[83]. E.R. Ruspini, "New experimental results in fuzzy clustering", Information Sciences, Vol.6, Pp.273–284, 1973.

[84]. M.Ryoke, Y. Nakamori and K. Suzuki, "Adaptive fuzzy clustering and fuzzy prediction models", Fuzzy Systems, 1995.

[85]. G. Salton, "Introduction to Modern Information Retrieval", McGraw-Hill, 1983.

[86]. G. Salton and C. Buckley, "Term Weighting Approaches in Automatic Text Retrieval", Information Processing and Management, Vol.24, No.5, Pp.513–523, 1988.

[87]. G. Salton,"An Introduction to Modern Information Retrieval", McGraw Hill, 1983.

[88]. Sayantani Ghosh, Sudipta Roy and Samir K. Bandyopadhyay, "A tutorial review on Text Mining Algorithms", International Journal of Advanced Research in Computer and Communication Engineering, Vol.1, No.4, 2002.

[89]. S.Z.Selim and M.A. Ismail, "k-Means-type algorithms: A generalized convergence theorem and characterization of local optimality", IEEE Transactions on Pattern Analysis and Machine Intelligence, Vol.6, No.1, Pp.81–87, 1984.

[90]. A.V. Senthilkumar and S.M. Jagatheesan, "An Efficient approach for Mining Frequesnt Item sets", Proceedings of I[st] International Conference on Data Engineering and Management, Pp.47-49, 2008.

[91]. G.Sheikholeslami, S.Chatterjee and Z. Hang, "A Wave Cluster: A multi-resolution clustering approach for very large spatial data bases", VLDB, 1998.

[92]. J. Shi and J. Malik, "Normalized Cuts and Image Segmentation", IEEE Transactions on Pattern Analysis and Machine Intelligence, Vol.22, No.8, Pp.888-905, 2000.

[93]. K. Sikka, N. Sinha, P.K. Singh and A.K. Mishra, "A Fully Automated Algorithm under Modified FCM Framework for Improved Brain MR Image Segmentation", Magnetic Resonance Imaging, Vol.27, No.7, Pp.994–1004, 2009.

[94]. M.Sips, B. Neubert, J.P. Lewis and P.Hanrahan, "Selecting good views of high-dimensional data using class consistency", Computer Graphics Forum, Vol.28, No.3, Pp.831–838, 2009.

[95]. SudiptoGuha, Rajeev Rastogi and Kyuseok Shim, "ROCK: A Robust Clustering Algorithm for Categorical Attributes", Proceedings of the 15th International Conference on Data Engineering, Pp.512-521, 1999.

[96]. Sudipto Guha, Rajeev Rastogi and Kyuseok Shim, "CURE: A clustering algorithm for large databases", Proceeding of the ACM SIGMOD Conference on Management of Data, 1998.

[97]. M. Sabeghi and M. Naghibzadeh, "A Fuzzy Algorithm for Real-Time Scheduling of Soft Periodic Tasks", IJCSNS International Journal of Computer Science and Network Security, Vol.6, No.2, 2006.

[98]. M. Sugeno, "Industrial applications of fuzzy control", Elsevier Science Inc. New York, NY, 1985.

[99]. Takashi Washio, Hiroki Matsuura and Hiroshi Motoda, "Mining association rules for estimation and prediction", Research and Development in Knowledge Discovery and Data Mining Lecture Notes in Computer Science, Vol.1394, Pp.417-419, 1998.

[100]. Thomas H. Cormen, Charles E. Leiserson and Ronald L. Rivest, "Introduction to Algorithms", MIT Press, Massachusetts, 1990.

[101]. A. Topchy, A.K. Jain and W. Punch, "Combining Multiple Weak Clustering", Proceedings of the IEEE International Conference on Data Mining, USA, Pp.331-338, 2003.

[102]. C.J. Van Rijsbergen. "Information Retrieval", Butterworth, 1975.

[103]. W. Wang, J. Yang and R. Muntz, "STING: A statistical information grid approach to spatial data mining", VLDB, Vol.97, Pp.186-195, 1997.

[104]. L.X. Wang, "A course in fuzzy systems and control", Prentice Hall, Paperback, 1996.

[105]. J. Wilbur and K. Sirotkin, "The automatic identification of stop words", Journal of Information Science, Vol.18, Pp.45–55, 1992.

[106]. Y. Yang and J.O. Pederson, "A comparative study on feature selection in text categorization", ACM SIGIR Conference, 1995.

[107]. D.Q. Zhang and S.C. Chen, "A Novel Kernelized Fuzzy C-Means Algorithm With Application in Medical Image Segmentation", Artificial Intelligence Med, Vol.32, Pp.37–50, 2004.

[108]. T. Zhang, R. Ramakrishnan and M. Livny, "BIRCH: An Efficient Data Clustering Method for Very Large Databases", ACM SIGMOD Conference, 1996.

[109]. Zhexue Huang, "Extensions to the k-Means Algorithm for Clustering Large Data Sets with Categorical Values", Data Mining and Knowledge Discovery, Vol.2, No.3, Pp.283-304, 1998.

[110]. Zoubin Ghahramani, "Unsupervised Learning", Advanced Lectures on Machine Learning LNAI 3174, 2004.

[111]. Oracle Data warehousing guide–Release 2(9.2)

[112]. CompRef8/Data Warehouse Design: Modern Principles and Methodologies/Golfarelli & Rizzi/039-1

[113]. The quotations are taken from http://www.famousquotesandauthors.com, 2012.